Skewer It!

Mary Corpening Barber

Sara Corpening Whiteford

with Rebecca Chastenet de Géry

Photographs by Leigh Beisch

Skewer It!

50 Recipes for Stylish Entertaining

CHRONICLE BOOKS

SAN FRANCISCO

Library of Congress Cataloging-in-Publication Data available.

ISBN 0-8118-2815-8

Printed in Hong Kong.

Prop stylist: Sara Slavin
Food stylist: Dan Becker
Photographer's assistant:
Sheri Giblin
Food stylist's assistant:
Jonathan Justus

Design: Pamela Geismar
Fonts: Rockwell, Spectrum
Dingbats: Linotype Decoration Pi

Toblerone, Nutella, and Kellogg's Rice Krispies are registered trademarks.

Distributed in Canada by
Raincoast Books
9050 Shaughnessy Street
Vancouver, B.C. V6P 6E5

10 9 8 7 6 5 4 3 2 1

Chronicle Books LLC
85 Second Street
San Francisco, California 94105

www.chroniclebooks.com

Acknowledgments

We thank Rebecca Chastenet de Géry for her significant contribution in the way of words. She delivered zest and fervor to the text of this book, as well as tremendous enthusiasm for the expansive realm of skewered foods. We are grateful for her sound advice, and for her reliable insights into cooking, entertaining, and food presentation.

We also want to thank our loving and food-adoring family for their honesty and constructive criticism, specifically Jack and Erik, our wonderful husbands. And to our valued friends and recipe testers, we appreciate your comments and queries, which have helped us to create friendlier recipes that are more accurate and more time-efficient: Liza Williams, Victoria Reid, Laura Heppert, Libit Schoch, Andrea Madruga, Marta Bosco, Patricia Willets, Katherine Cobbs, Susan Corpening, Carter Foster, Sierra Gehrke, Lucy Bowen, and Bruce Taylor. Last but not least, a big thanks to Tori Ritchie, and the gang at Chronicle Books, especially Bill LeBlond.

We would also like to thank Janet Torelli, Niki Stix, Fillamento, Handblock, Hermes Vieau Design, and Crate & Barrel for their generous contributions of the skewers used in the photography. See "Resources" on page 114 for more information.

Contents

INTRODUCTION 8
TIPS AND TECHNIQUES FOR THREADED FOODS II
TYPES OF SKEWERS I3
MENU IDEAS FOR SKEWERED OCCASIONS 16
INGREDIENT GLOSSARY I7

FESTIVE FINGER FOODS AND PARTY PICKS
Moroccan-Spiced Swordfish with Red Peppers and Lemon Drizzle 27
Mushrooms and Sweet Pearl Onions with Cabernet Syrup 28
Apple Wood–Smoked Bacon-Wrapped Scallops with Tamari Glaze 30
Chicken with Chutney and Macadamia Nuts 32
Balsamic Sun-Dried Tomatoes, Broccoli, and Smoked Gouda 33
Lamb with Mint-Mustard Dipping Sauce 34
Eggplant, Chèvre, and Mint Rolls 35
Cold Chicken, Mint, and Cucumbers with Fiery Mango Dipping Sauce 36
Glazed Shrimp with Bourbon Barbecue Dunk 39
Lobster and Asparagus with Lemony Tarragon Aioli 40
Beef Satay 42
Smoked Turkey, Avocado, and Bacon with Blue Cheese Vinaigrette 43
Peppery Bacon-Wrapped Watermelon Rind Pickles 44
New Potatoes with Three-Cheese Fondue 45
Spicy Tofu with Cilantro and Smoky Black Bean Dip 47
Tuna with Black Olives and Marinated Artichoke Crowns 48
Spinach Tortellini with Roasted Red Pepper Pesto 49
Lacquered Pork with Water Chestnuts and Snow Peas 5I
Open-Faced Mini Reubens 52
Roasted Yellow Squash and Zucchini with Green Onion and Basil Dip 53
And Other Crudité Combos 54
Kielbasa and Potatoes with Caraway-Honey Mustard 55
Sesame-Crusted Salmon with Pineapple-Miso Sauce 56
Smoked Duck with Spiced Apricots and Watercress 58

NONCOOK CONCOCTIONS
Melon, Prosciutto, and Arugula with Lime–Poppy Seed Vinaigrette 6I
Spanish Olive and Cream Cheese Spheres on Red Pepper Squares 62
Curried Pimiento Cheese and Spinach Pinwheels 63
Cherry Tomatoes, Marinated Artichoke Hearts, and Mozzarella 64
Smoked Salmon, Cream Cheese, and Martini Onion Roulades 66
Salami, Pepperoncini, and Jack Cheese with Lemon-Oregano Essence 67

KABOBS REVISITED: BIG, BOLD, AND DELICIOUS

Chicken Fondue with Sun-Dried Tomato Aioli and Curry Sauce   69
Caesar Salad with Lemongrass-Skewered Shrimp and Scallops   70
Mahimahi, Pineapple, and Bell Pepper Brochettes with Cilantro Sauce   73
Lamb, Figs, and Lemon Confit with Mint-Yogurt Dipping Sauce   74
London Broil, Yellow Bell Pepper, Shiitake, and Red Onion Kabobs   77
Pinwheel Steaks with Basil-Parsley Pesto and Roasted Red Peppers   79
Spiced Pork with Plums, Roasted Garlic, and Bay Leaves   81
Mushroom, Red Pepper, and Squash Yakitori   82

SWEET-TOOTH SATISFIERS

Honeydew, Mint, and Kiwis with Lime-Yogurt Dipping Sauce   87
Mini Ice-Cream Sandwiches with Raspberries   88
Glazed Strawberry Shortcakes with Lemony Sour Cream   90
Coconut Tapioca Custard with Tropical Fruits and Apricot Syrup   92
Chocolate-Covered Banana Sicles with Peanut Sprinkles   94
Cantaloupe and Blackberry Skewers with Raspberry-Crème Swirl   95
Fudge Brownies with Miniature Candy Canes   97
White Toblerone Fondue with Kiwi and Pineapple Picks   98

KID STIX

County Fair Corn Dogs   100
Caramel Apples   101
Sweet Potato and Marshmallow Stix   102
Watermelon and Blueberry Popsicles   104
Peanut Butter, Rice Krispie, and Chocolate Chip Roll-ups   105

COCKTAILS AND SWIZZLES

Bloody Marys   107
Frozen Strawberry Daiquiris   108
Margaritas   109
Martinis   109
Cosmopolitans   111
Manhattans   111
Piña Coladas   112
Sangria Smoothies   112

RESOURCES   114
INDEX   115
TABLE OF EQUIVALENTS   120

Introduction

Put it on a pick, thread it on a stick, pierce it, wrap it, roll it—skewer it! Playful, practical, yet sophisticated and explosively flavorful, today's skewers are a far cry from the shish kabobs that formerly starred in suburban backyards. Flip through these pages, and you'll discover a whole new world of skewered food. Our recipes go way beyond standard kabobs and fondue. They break culinary barriers and challenge you to stack up textures, flavors, and colors in an innovative way.

With their endless flavor combinations, skewers speak to a new culinary generation, one that demands global tastes prepared in little time and presented in a way that excites the imagination. Finger food takes on new meaning when skewers come into play. Almost any ingredient is fair game, and because skewered foods can be cooked on the stovetop, in the oven, or served straight from the fridge, you don't need a grill to make them. Think meat. Think seafood. Think vegetables. Think dessert. Then start mixing, matching, and spearing, and you're headed in the right direction.

One part nostalgia (remember corn dogs and roasted marshmallows?), one part cutting edge (consider Moroccan-Spiced Swordfish with Red Peppers and Lemon Drizzle), skewers breathe new life into the party scene. Presentation is more than half the equation when entertaining, and with skewers, you get great taste and good looks all wrapped into one. With minimum effort, skewers allow cuisines from around the world to converge on the same table, offering manageable mouthfuls of delicious discovery. Skewer a food that lacks luster, like crudités, boiled shrimp, or brownies, and revel in its transformation into a hip, inspired dish.

Clean, clever, and undeniably sexy, skewers send the imagination soaring and invite innovation. Take our Mini Ice-Cream Sandwiches with Raspberries. Served conventionally, ice-cream sandwiches may fail to excite, but cut into bite-sized bits, dusted with rich cocoa powder, and crowned with red raspberries, they earn innumerable oohs and ahs.

As you turn the pages of *Skewer It!,* you'll discover that these creative meals and sumptuous snacks stacked smartly on a stick defy categorization. In the cocktail vein, you'll find substantial hors d'oeuvres like our Lacquered Pork with Water Chestnuts and Snow Peas, as well as lighter offerings like our Cold Chicken, Mint, and Cucumbers with Fiery Mango Dipping Sauce. Seafood fans will do flips over our festive spears of Glazed Shrimp with Bourbon Barbecue

Dunk and our succulent Apple Wood–Smoked Bacon-Wrapped Scallops with Tamari Glaze, while those with a vegetarian bent will relish combinations like our tri-colored skewer of Balsamic Sun-Dried Tomatoes, Broccoli, and Smoked Gouda and our refreshing Eggplant, Chèvre, and Mint Rolls. When you're pressed for time, our "noncook" recipes for party nibbles beat peanuts and pretzels any day. Imagine Spanish Olive and Cream Cheese Spheres on Red Pepper Squares, or Salami, Pepperoncini, and Jack Cheese with Lemon-Oregano Essence.

Full-meal deals are included in *Skewer It!* too. Begin with our Caesar Salad with Lemongrass-Skewered Shrimp and Scallops or our Pinwheel Steaks with Basil-Parsley Pesto and Roasted Red Pepper. Conclude dinner with a speared dessert of Glazed Strawberry Shortcakes with Lemony Sour Cream or Coconut Tapioca Custard with Tropical Fruits and Apricot Syrup.

And we haven't forgotten the kids. Our chapter dedicated to the little ones in your life was written with their finicky taste buds in mind. In it, you'll discover easy-to-achieve recipes for corn dogs, caramel apples, and a delightful snack-time roll-up laden with protein-packed peanut butter and sinful chocolate chips.

Simply doing drinks? You still need *Skewer It!* Your guests will go berserk over our swanky swizzle sticks stacked with cocktail-appropriate garnish combinations. Showcase them at the bar or place them right in the glass to create highballs loaded with high style.

Simple, straightforward, yet so novel in their approach, the recipes in *Skewer It!* plant you firmly on the culinary frontier. With *Skewer It!,* creating a unique eating experience is assured. Go ahead. Take a stab at skewering your food.

Tips and Techniques for Threaded Foods

SOAKING WOODEN SKEWERS

We recommend soaking wooden (bamboo) skewers for about 30 minutes before assembling our recipes in order to prevent splintering and/or burning. Toothpicks are an exception; they won't splinter. However, if you intend to cook foods on toothpicks, soak them first or they will burn.

SIZES AND SHAPES

We've included precise measurements for ingredients in our recipes, and it's not because we're big fans of the ruler or the measuring cup. It's just that after years in the catering business, we've noticed a general tendency to serve bigger-than-necessary portions, which makes for awkward "grazing." In our recipes, particularly those found in the finger foods chapter, we've intentionally called for small, bite-sized skewer ingredients. Keeping portions small creates more approachable finger food. The last thing you want to do is serve over-sized hors d'oeuvres that intimidate rather than tempt. With regard to dinner-sized kabobs, our measurements were created with cooking in mind. Uniformity of shape allows for the most even cooking. Follow our preparation instructions as closely as possible for optimum results.

DON'T OVERLOAD YOUR SKEWERS

There's nothing less appealing than an hors d'oeuvre that doubles as a choking hazard! When assembling skewers, make sure you thread your ingredients on the tip of the stick so that the pointed end is barely visible. Ask yourself, with each skewer you string, if you've created a manageable mouthful. We designed our recipes to feed your guests, not to gag them!

RECEPTACLES

Whether you're serving skewers as passed hors d'oeuvres or from platters on a buffet table, you'll need a container for collecting used sticks. A demitasse cup is ideal for toothpicks, whereas a champagne flute or an unusual vase makes an attractive receptacle for used skewers. Place a used skewer in the cup, glass, or vase prior to serving your guests and they will follow suit.

COOKING TO PERFECTION

You don't have to own a grill to turn out wonderful skewers. But owning a grill or a grill pan is a plus, because grilling gives wonderful flavor and a great look to most foods. If you do choose to use an outdoor grill for cooking skewers, be sure to check them frequently. Wooden skewers, quite obviously, are highly flammable. While soaking the skewers does reduce the risk of their catching fire, dripping fat from foods might nonetheless cause them to ignite. Our word to the wise: Don't walk away from your grill. You might return to skewers reduced to ash.

As far as grill pans go, they work best for cooking dinner-sized skewers because the skewer tips don't touch the hot grill surface. We've had problems cooking finger-food skewers in grill pans because the picks tend to come into direct contact with the heat and burn. Grill pans also work well for recipes that call for grilling ingredients prior to skewering, because you won't have to worry about small pieces of food falling through a grill rack.

When cooking skewers in the oven or under the broiler, keep a close eye on them as well. Although we've given detailed cooking instructions, all ovens are different, and many are not properly calibrated. If you notice your skewers are getting too dark too fast, shift them to a lower oven rack, cover them with aluminum foil, or lower the oven temperature.

Types of Skewers

A variety of objects can be used to spear foods, from traditional bamboo skewers to edible ones like candy canes. Some skewers, like rosemary sprigs, add both flavor and interest to food. By all means, don't limit skewered items to toothpicks. Here is a listing of earthy, elegant, practical, and sophisticated skewers.

ROSEMARY

This tough, woody herb is a natural for skewering, not only because of its aesthetic appeal, but because it perfumes the food it holds. Choose sturdy rosemary sprigs and remember that the sprig, particularly the featherlike tip, will wilt when cooked. Strip off the leaves at the base of the sprig (to make skewering easier) and soak the sprigs in water for at least 15 minutes prior to exposing them to heat.

LEMONGRASS

The stiff stalk of this flavorful Asian herb makes a sleek skewer. Before using, trim the lemongrass, removing all dried, brownish leaves. To use the base of a lemongrass stalk, slice it at an angle to create a sharp point. The more slender upper portion of the stalk can also be used for skewering. Soak lemongrass for at least 15 minutes before cooking.

SUGARCANE

Both the fresh and canned versions of this sweet spear create a unique skewer, although canned sugarcane is more widely available and is easier to cut into skewers. If you do locate fresh sugarcane, peel the stalks and carefully slice them into ¼-inch-thick lengths. Canned sugarcane stalks are generally ¾ inch to an inch in diameter. For best results, cut them into several skewers about ¼ inch thick.

CINNAMON STICKS

Long cinnamon sticks (about 6 inches long) used as skewers are sure to enchant children, and their blunt ends are conveniently "child-proof" as well. As a general rule, the thinner the cinnamon stick, the better. Thick sticks can cause food to break during assembly. Long cinnamon sticks are available at most natural foods stores and specialty grocers. They may also be ordered from Penzey's

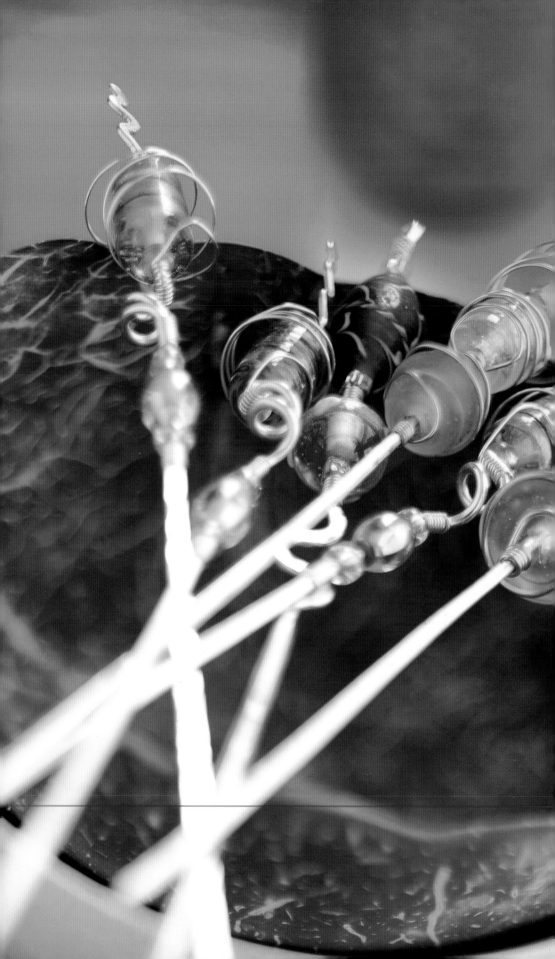

Spices at 800-741-7787 or from their website: www.penzeys.com (4 ounces amounts to fifteen 6-inch sticks).

CANDY CANES

For a breath-freshening skewered dessert, look for pencil-thin canes no more than 3 inches long. Food skewered on candy canes must be substantial enough to be skewered by a cane without breaking. Fudge brownies are the perfect match for these sweet sticks.

DRINKING STRAWS

Long or short, colorful or clear, thick or thin—we love them just about any way! Straws make great skewers because they invite imagination. We think they're at their best as fruit skewers and skewers for kids, but they're also great gussied up as drink swizzles.

WOODEN SKEWERS

Wooden skewers made from bamboo range in size from 6 to 12 inches long. We vary the length of the skewer according to the dish and the occasion, and give specific measurements for skewers in our recipes. But don't fret if you can't get the exact size. The longer skewers are more readily available and can be substituted for the shorter skewers, or simply cut to size with sturdy scissors. Remember to soak wooden skewers before using. Popsicle sticks and wooden dowels are better skewers for children because of their blunt tips.

DECORATIVE SKEWERS

The decorative skewer market is growing by leaps and bounds. We've spotted stainless-steel chopsticks, hand-painted lacquered chopsticks, and beaded sterling silver skewers in shops around San Francisco, not to mention the array of swizzle sticks, colored wood skewers, and plastic picks that add a decorative quality to skewered foods. Be forewarned that many decorative skewers, while beautiful, should not be heated, so choose recipes that involve no direct heat to showcase these pretty picks. Or, cook the skewered ingredients first and assemble them to serve.

STAINLESS STEEL VS. CHROME VS. NONSTICK

We've seen and used them all. Chrome skewers will rust with time, so we recommend paying a little more for their stainless-steel counterparts. Stainless-steel skewers, which are dishwasher safe, have either flat or round blades. We prefer flat spears because they prevent foods from spinning on the skewer while cooking. Nonstick skewers are practical and pretty. They are easy to clean, too.

Ever thought about having a skewer party? We've catered countless theme parties over the years and are always on the lookout for something new. Let this be your guide for skewer soirees.

FONDUE PARTY *for 12*

New Potatoes with Three-Cheese
    Fondue (3 x recipe)
Chicken Fondue with Sun-Dried
    Tomato Aioli and Curry Sauce
    (3 x recipe)
White Toblerone Fondue with Kiwi
    and Pineapple Picks (1½ x recipe)
*We recommend serving this dinner with
    a side salad and French bread.*
Suggested Cocktail: Manhattans

SEATED DINNER *for 8*

Eggplant, Chèvre, and Mint Rolls
    (1 recipe)
Pinwheel Steaks with Basil-Parsley
    Pesto and Roasted Red Peppers
    (2 x recipe)
Mushrooms and Sweet Pearl Onions
    with Cabernet Syrup (2 x recipe)
White Toblerone Fondue with Kiwi
    and Pineapple Picks (1 recipe)
    (substitute milk chocolate for
    white chocolate in this recipe, if
    you desire, and vary the dipping
    ingredients)
Suggested Cocktail: Martinis

"GRAZING-STYLE" DINNER

    (all finger foods) *for 24*
Beef Satay (2 x recipe)
Chicken with Chutney and
    Macadamia Nuts (2 x recipe)
Moroccan-Spiced Swordfish with
    Red Peppers and Lemon Drizzle
    (2 x recipe)
Spinach Tortellini with Roasted Red
    Pepper Pesto (2 x recipe)

Roasted Yellow Squash and Zucchini
    with Green Onion and Basil Dip
    (2 x recipe)
Suggested Cocktail: Cosmopolitans

PRE-DINNER COCKTAIL PARTY *for 24*

Lamb with Mint-Mustard Dipping
    Sauce (2 x recipe)
Balsamic Sun-Dried Tomatoes,
    Broccoli, and Smoked Gouda
    (2 x recipe)
Suggested Cocktail: Manhattans

SEATED LUNCHEON *for 8*

Cold Chicken, Mint, and Cucumbers
    with Fiery Mango Dipping Sauce
    (1 recipe)
Melon, Prosciutto, and Arugula with
    Lime–Poppy Seed Vinaigrette
    (1 recipe)
Caesar Salad with Lemongrass-
    Skewered Shrimp and Scallops
    (2 x recipe)
Coconut Tapioca Custard with
    Tropical Fruits and Apricot
    Syrup (1 recipe)
Suggested Cocktail: Bloody Marys

COUNTY FAIR SUPPER *for 8*

    (4 adults, 4 kids)
Open-Faced Mini Reubens (1 recipe)
Spinach Tortellini with Roasted Red
    Pepper Pesto (1 recipe)
County Fair Corn Dogs (1½ x recipe)
Caramel Apples (1 recipe)
*We recommend serving with macaroni
    and cheese or coleslaw.*
Suggested Cocktail: Sangria Smoothies
    (for the adults); Piña Coladas
    (nonalcoholic version) for the
    kids

BALSAMIC VINEGAR: An exquisite Italian specialty vinegar made from barrel-aged white Trebbiano grape juice, balsamic vinegar is low in acid, sweet, and surprisingly complex in flavor. Balsamic gives intensity to salad dressings and marinades and is great drizzled over fruit. Quality counts. Buy the finest balsamic vinegar you can afford.

CHAMPAGNE VINEGAR: As its name indicates, champagne vinegar is made from champagne, as opposed to the more common red-wine base. Mild in flavor, it is readily available in supermarkets.

CHILI SAUCE: This ketchuplike blend of tomatoes, vinegar, corn syrup, salt, onions, and garlic does wonders for burgers and fries, but given its brighter, sharper flavor, we think it gives ketchup a run for its money!

CHIPOTLE CHILES IN ADOBO SAUCE: These smoked, dried jalapeño chiles taste sweet, smoky, and almost chocolatey and possess a decidedly fiery kick. Available dried, pickled, or canned in adobo sauce—a blend of dried chiles, water, salt, and sugar—chipotles can be found in the Mexican food section of grocery stores or at Latino markets.

CHUTNEY: We can't imagine a pantry without chutney, a sprightly condiment made of fruit and spices that varies in flavor, texture, and heat. Major Grey's, one of our favorite styles of mango chutney, has the balance of sugar, spice, and tang we adore. Pick up a jar in the ethnic food aisle of your grocery store. It's a sure-fire way to add zip to ordinary dishes.

COCONUT EXTRACT: Extracts are concentrated flavorings captured from foods or plants, usually through evaporation or distillation. They impact flavor without adding volume or altering consistency. Coconut extract often bears the label "imitation," which means a little dab will do. (Add too much, and your creation will taste more of suntan lotion than real coconut!) Though we usually balk at anything "imitation," we make an exception here—a drop of coconut extract provides great depth to smoothies, tapioca, and custards.

COCONUT MILK: You would think that coconut milk was milk gleaned from fresh coconuts, but this isn't the case. Instead, it's made from a mixture of equal parts water and shredded fresh coconut that is simmered until foamy, then strained through cheesecloth. Coconut cream, which is thicker and usually sweetened, is produced in a similar fashion, using one part water to four parts coconut meat. Don't confuse coconut milk with sweetened "cream of coconut," which is used in desserts and tropical drinks.

COCKTAIL ONIONS: Also known as Martini or pearl onions, these diminutive bulbs can do so much more than merely garnish your Gibson. Use them as a garnish for foods. They add zip and crunch to otherwise ordinary concoctions. Shop for quality when purchasing cocktail onions. We've noticed that the cheaper brands are more astringent, while the higher-quality ones are more balanced in flavor, making them a better bet for seasoning foods.

CRÈME FRAÎCHE: This velvety, rich, "mature" cream is more voluptuous and less sour than sour cream. One beautiful thing about crème fraîche is that it won't curdle when boiled. Commercial brands are widely available, although crème fraîche can be made at home by combining 1 cup whipping cream with 2 tablespoons buttermilk in a bowl. Let the mixture sit at room temperature (about 70°F) for 8 to 24 hours until it thickens. Stir thoroughly, cover, and refrigerate for up to 10 days.

DRY MUSTARD: One of the oldest culinary and medicinal spices, mustard comes in many forms. Dry mustard is made from ground mustard seeds, and gives zest to sauces, rubs, salad dressings, and marinades. Store it in a dry, dark place for up to 6 months.

FISH SAUCE: Don't be alarmed by the pungent odor of fish sauce, also known as fish gravy—it's a dynamite condiment. Popular throughout Southeast Asia, fish sauce is made from various mixtures of salted, fermented fish. Asian markets carry a wide variety of fish sauces, including Thai, Vietnamese, Filipino, and Japanese. Also look for this condiment in the Asian foods section of supermarkets.

FIVE-SPICE POWDER: What we love about Chinese five-spice powder is its all-in-one flavor advantage. The Chinese use this pungent blend of cinnamon, cloves, fennel seeds, star anise, and Szechwan peppercorns with extravagance, much as the Indians employ curry blends. Five-spice powder is an easy spice to abuse, however. A tiny amount offers big, bold flavor. Sold in nearly every Asian market, five-spice powder is also available in the spice section of most supermarkets.

FROZEN JUICE CONCENTRATES: Concentrated juices such as cranberry, pineapple, and white grape add intense flavor to sauces and glazes, along with a healthy dose of vitamin C. Their high acidity also makes them an attractive addition to marinades, where they act as tenderizers as well as flavor boosters.

GHERKINS AND CORNICHONS: The difference? Cornichons are miniature French versions of the green gherkin cucumbers grown especially for making pickles. Crisp and tart, they are usually sold in jars, packed in a vinegar solution flavored with salt and spices.

GREEN CURRY PASTE: This spirited paste is a mixture of green chiles, garlic, onion, salt, and spices. We are particularly fond of Thai Kitchen brand curry paste, which is available in the Asian section of most supermarkets or from Epicurean International (call 800-967-8424 for purchasing information, or visit Epicurean's website at www.thaikitchen.com).

HARISSA: Harissa is to couscous what wasabi is to sushi. This fiery paste hails from Northern Africa (Morocco, Tunisia, and Algeria) and features chiles, garlic, cumin, coriander, and olive oil. The traditional couscous condiment, harissa also enhances hearty soups and stews. It can be found in cans, jars, and tubes in most Middle Eastern markets. If you dab a little of this exotic chile paste directly on your tongue (which is what we did when we tasted it for the first time), we promise you you'll never forget it!

HOISIN: Ever since we discovered Peking duck in Chinese restaurants as little girls, we've insisted on keeping this close at hand. The Chinese equivalent to ketchup, this ultra-thick, reddish-brown sauce is served mainly as a table condiment, but also acts as a flavor enhancer for meat and seafood dishes. Known also as Peking sauce, this salty, sweet, slightly sour mixture contains soybeans, garlic, chiles, and spices. After opening, hoisin should be refrigerated. It will keep indefinitely. If you purchase hoisin in a can, be sure to transfer it to a nonmetal container and seal it tightly.

HORSERADISH: Consider horseradish as a lively radish with the heat factor multiplied ten-fold. Two types are widely available. One is prepared horseradish, which is a comparatively mild blend of horseradish and mayonnaise found in jars in the condiment aisle of your grocery. The other, our favorite, is fresh horseradish preserved in vinegar. It comes refrigerated and is often located in the kosher section of supermarkets. Fresh horse-radish roots are available in the spring at specialty produce markets. Seize the opportunity to make your own horseradish sauce.

KOSHER SALT: We call for kosher salt in all of our recipes because we like its bright, clean flavor. Kosher salt is free of additives and has a wonderfully coarse texture that makes it ideal for adding to food in pinches. If you are wedded to plain table salt or iodized salt (which is table salt with added iodine), simply use half the amount called for in our recipes (1 teaspoon kosher salt equals ½ teaspoon iodized salt). Sea salt, which costs a bit more, has become the rage of the food world. It packs great flavor and is available in a variety of textures, from the finest *fleur de sel*, used as a final seasoning, to the coarser *sel gris.* Because of the wealth of textures available, sea salt equivalents are difficult to give.

LEMONGRASS: A signature herb in Thai cuisine, lemongrass is also referred to as citronella and sereh. This long, thin, grassy spear has a bulbous base similar to that of a scallion and a delicate lemon flavor without the sourness. Usually steeped in liquid, lemongrass infuses teas, broths, and soups with a subtle citrus note. Strain the lemongrass from the liquid following infusion, as its coarse texture is not palatable. The herb is available both fresh and dried in Asian markets, although fresh lemongrass has considerably more flavor. Lemongrass can be frozen successfully.

LIME (OR LEMON) ZEST: The zest is the aromatic outer skin of citrus fruits. The essential oils within the zest impart great flavor, but beware of the white pith found just underneath it. The pith is exceptionally bitter and should not be used in cooking. A zester efficiently removes thin shreds of zest without the pith, although you can also use a fine cheese grater.

MIRIN: A staple in Japanese cuisine, this low-alcohol wine, often referred to as rice wine, is made from glutinous rice. Syrupy and sweet, it adds dimension to numerous dishes, sauces, and glazes and can be found at Asian specialty markets and in the gourmet section of most grocery stores.

MISO: An essential ingredient in Japanese cooking, miso is a thick paste of fermented soybeans loaded with B vitamins and protein. Three basic types of miso exist on the market: barley, rice, and soybean. All three are made by injecting cooked soybeans with a mold called koji, which is cultivated in a base of barley, rice, or soybeans. Like cheeses, misos undergo aging, most from six months to three years. In general, light-colored misos are more delicate than darker versions (misos range from yellow to reddish brown to dark brown). Experiment with the different types to determine your preference. Miso is located in the refrigerated section of Asian markets and in many natural foods and specialty stores.

OLIVE OIL: Cherished for centuries in the Mediterranean region, olive oil has become a permanent fixture in most American kitchens. The multitude of olive oils on the market, however, can lead to confusion. Note that the flavor, color, fragrance, and acidity of olive oil varies dramatically depending on its growing region and pressing style. Extra-virgin olive oil comes from the first cold pressing of the olives and has an acidity level below 1 percent, making it the finest, fruitiest, and most expensive of olive oils. It should not be used for high-heat cooking because of its low smoking point and is best employed as a finishing agent. (In the European community, olive oil is not only graded by its acidity level, but by a panel of highly trained official tasters. California olive oil is not yet graded by such a panel.) Virgin olive oil possesses a slightly higher level of acidity, ranging from 1 to 3 percent, and is typically less fruity than extra-virgin oil. Light olive oil has little of the classic olive-oil flavor due to its extremely fine filtration but is not any lower in calories. It is ideal for high-heat cooking methods, such as pan-frying, sautéing, or deep-frying, because of its high smoking point. Light olive oil may also be used in baking because of its mild flavor.

PIMIENTO: You may never have come face to face with fresh pimiento, but no doubt you have experienced this racy red pepper as an olive stuffing, a colorful accent to shredded cheese, or in its dried ground form called paprika. Often confused with red bell peppers, pimientos are heart-shaped sweet peppers that tend to be more aromatic than the bell. Due to their short growing season and restricted availability, we rely on pimientos in jars for use as a quick, easy garnish.

POPPY SEEDS: These diminutive seeds of the poppy plant have a crunchy texture and nutty flavor. High in oil content, they are especially prone to rancidity, so store them in an airtight container in the refrigerator for no longer than 6 months. Toasting poppy seeds lightly over low heat in a dry skillet augments their flavor.

RICE VINEGAR: This fermented rice vinegar, a fixture in Japanese cooking, is mild, low in acidity, and slightly sweet. It comes both "seasoned" and plain. We prefer the seasoned version. If you are unable to find seasoned rice vinegar, add 1 tablespoon sugar and ¾ tablespoon kosher salt to ¼ cup unseasoned rice vinegar for an acceptable substitute. Some brown rice vinegars on the market are cherished by connoisseurs in the same way as many of the finest balsamic vinegars are. Look for both products in Asian markets and at most standard grocery stores.

ROASTED RED PEPPERS: Freshly roasted red peppers packed in jars in oil or in their own juices are readily available in supermarkets. Although they are an acceptable substitute for home-roasted peppers, we prefer to make our own. To roast peppers, trim their ends and cut each pepper in half lengthwise. Remove their seeds and

ribs, and place the peppers skin-side up on an aluminum-foil-lined baking sheet. Brush them liberally with oil and roast in a preheated 350°F oven for about 30 minutes, or until the peppers are soft (note that their skins do not blacken and blister, as they do with direct-heat methods). Transfer to a bowl and cover it with plastic wrap. When cool to the touch, gently remove the peppers' skins.

SAKE: In Japan, this wine traditionally arrives at the table warm in little porcelain cups. Slightly sweet, with a relatively low alcohol content of 12 to 16 percent, sake is made from fermented rice and is used in cooking to enhance sauces, glazes, and marinades.

SESAME OIL: There are two types of sesame oil: dark and light. Use dark Asian sesame oil (made from toasted sesame seeds) in cautiously small doses. Its pungent flavor is particularly well suited to Asian-inspired preparations. Light sesame oil has a delicate, nutty flavor. It is exceptionally versatile and can be used in anything from dressings to high-heat cooking methods, such as sautéing and stir-frying, given its elevated smoking point.

SESAME SEEDS: These tiny seeds come in many colors: black, white, red, and brown. For aesthetic reasons, we use black and white sesame seeds tossed together. White sesame seeds are sold hulled (pure white) and unhulled (gray brown). The unhulled seeds have a more pronounced flavor. Because of their high oil content, sesame seeds turn rancid quickly. Store them in the refrigerator in an airtight container for up to 6 months, or freeze them for up to 1 year. White sesame seeds are common in the United States. The less-common black sesame seeds, prominent in Chinese and Japanese cooking, can be found in Asian markets. To order via catalog, call Penzey's Spices at 800-741-7787, or consult their website: www.penzeys.com.

SHERRY: Sherry is a fortified wine that was originally made exclusively in Spain's Andalusia region. Now also produced in the United States, South Africa, and Australia, sherries vary in color, flavor, and sweetness from dry and light to dark, sweet, and creamy. Sherries vary in quality as well, from cheap mass-produced versions to connoisseur-quality limited editions. Our rule of thumb? Don't cook with a sherry you wouldn't drink!

SMOKED SALMON: When purchasing smoked salmon, by all means go for the high end. Many lower-end brands taste and smell a lot like cat food and will dramatically diminish the flavor of your recipe. Quality smoked salmon has a clean flavor and shouldn't taste or smell "fishy." There are two methods for smoking salmon. Hot-smoked salmon is smoked at 120° to 180°F for 6 to 12 hours. Cold-smoked salmon (the more common type), is smoked at 70° to 90°F for 1 day to up to 3 weeks. Lox is a brine-cured cold-smoked salmon that is often saltier than other smoked salmons.

TAMARI: Similar to soy sauce, but thicker and more complex in flavor, tamari is a mellow Asian condiment made from soybeans. Like soy, it makes a wonderful table condiment, a great dipping sauce, and excellent basting liquid. If you can't find tamari, substitute low-sodium soy sauce.

TAPIOCA: Extracted from cassava, a tropical plant, this starchy substance is sold in many forms from quick-cooking tapioca to pearl tapioca to tapioca flour. We prefer the quick-cooking variety, which is also the most readily available. Remember that the key to serving wonderful tapioca is getting the texture right. If overcooked, tapioca is like glue. Cook until just translucent and soft, and note that it will thicken as it cools. If, when chilled, the tapioca is overly thick, slowly stir in more milk.

TORTILLAS: The daily bread in many Latin American countries, tortillas exist in both corn and flour varieties. We call for flour tortillas in our recipes because they are sturdy yet pliable, making them ideal for wrapping and skewering. Flavored tortillas, such as tomato, spinach, and salsa varieties, are increasingly available in the Mexican foods section of supermarkets. Use them when available for an exceptionally vibrant presentation.

VEGETABLE SHORTENING: While testing meat fondue recipes, we discovered that shortening doesn't emit the strong odor that vegetable oil does when used for deep-frying. For this reason, we recommend shortening when you don't want your house to reek of frying oil. Vegetable shortenings are white, tasteless, and solid at room temperature. Avoid purchasing brands that contain artificial butter flavoring. Vegetable shortening can be stored at room temperature for up to 1 year.

WATER CHESTNUTS: There's nothing quite like a water chestnut. If you've never had the good fortune to devour a fresh one, make a trip to a Chinese market a top priority. We call for canned water chestnuts in this book since most people rely on these tasty alternatives. Mild in flavor and surprisingly crunchy, water chestnuts are the edible tubers of an aquatic plant indigenous to Southeast Asia. If you locate fresh ones, store them in the refrigerator for up to 1 week and peel their blackish-brownish skin before using.

WATERMELON RIND PICKLES: Although a staple in any Southern cook's kitchen, we've learned that many people "out West," "back East," and "up North" have never experienced these savory treats. The secret to cooking with the pickles is to make sure their flavor suits you from the outset. Some watermelon rind pickles are sweeter, crunchier, and spicier than others. We have a strong preference for pickles that aren't too sweet, with a pleasing tang and a subtle dose

of cinnamon, bay, and allspice. If we aren't the lucky recipients of our aunt's annual canning, we look for the Wood Stove Kitchens brand. The very best brands, typically, do not have corn syrup in the ingredient list.

WHITE TOBLERONE: This Swiss slice of heaven is a triangular bar of white chocolate accented with tidbits of nougat and hazelnut. We think these delectable little additions make for unparalleled fondue, but any high-quality white chocolate will work.

Festive Finger Foods and Party Picks

You've just opened up the biggest chapter in the book, loaded with unbeatable ideas for entertaining. It's no accident that we've developed nearly two dozen recipes for skewered finger foods. We've done so because we think skewers are at their best as cocktail food. Far more polished than an arbitrary selection of appetizers or hors d'oeuvres—not to mention far more fun—skewers allow you to layer flavors in neat, tidy packages sized just right for sampling in a single bite. Whether served as passed hors d'oeuvres, as plated appetizers, or from a buffet, these skewers are approachable and sexy. What's best, they offer an attractive way to graze.

Carnivores will find recipes for meat the way they like it: morsel after juicy morsel shamelessly stacked up in the center of the plate. Bold and bawdy alone, our meaty marvels take on more refined airs when paired with seductive sauces. Flirt with fire with our Cold Chicken, Mint, and Cucumbers with Fiery Mango Dipping Sauce. Succumb to the exotic with the dashing Beef Satay and its lively blend of coconut milk, peanut butter, green curry, and lime. Or abandon yourself to an earthy marriage of lamb, mustard, and mint.

If it's vegetables you're after, let our abundant larder of low-fat combinations entice you into a realm of healthy eating. We've layered textures, flavors, and colors for meatless dining that excites the senses. Curry and spinach dress up pimiento cheese for a contemporary take on an all-time favorite. Eggplant, chèvre, and mint join in an unforgettable trio of freshness. Smoked Gouda unexpectedly adds flair to broccoli and sun-dried tomatoes, and cilantro and black beans transform tofu into a culinary sensation. Even meat-lovers will be wooed by our substantial stack of mushrooms and sweet pearl onions draped in a robust Cabernet syrup.

For those times when you're fishing for something a little different, our seafood skewers promise a whole new wave of cocktail dining. Grazing goes luxurious with recipes for salmon, shrimp, tuna, and lobster. Dazzle dinner guests with our vibrant lobster and asparagus spear or our stellar combination of sesame-crusted salmon swirled in an exuberant pineapple-miso sauce. Spear tuna, kalamata olives, and artichoke hearts to create a splash at lunchtime. Or, pull out all the stops and prepare our entire seafood catch for your next party. Your guests won't believe their good fortune!

Moroccan-Spiced Swordfish with Red Peppers and Lemon Drizzle

Like the dizzying bazaars of Casablanca, this swordfish spear is awash with exotic flavors and aromas. The rich natural sugars of the red bell pepper, the astringency of the lemon, and the fiery harissa give this dish a three-dimensional balance. Most Middle Eastern specialty markets carry harissa, a hot Moroccan blend of red chiles, onions, garlic, and spices. If you can't locate this popular condiment, paprika and a pinch of cayenne make an acceptable replacement.

1½ teaspoons ground cumin
1½ teaspoons ground coriander
1 teaspoon paprika
¾ teaspoon kosher salt
1 tablespoon vegetable oil
Twenty-four ¾-inch cubes skinless,
    boneless swordfish (about
    12 ounces)

LEMON DRIZZLE:

1 tablespoon plus 2 teaspoons fresh
    lemon juice
2 teaspoons harissa, or ½ teaspoon
    paprika and a pinch of cayenne
1 teaspoon minced garlic
¼ teaspoon kosher salt
¼ teaspoon sugar
⅓ cup olive oil

Three ⅛-inch-thick lemon slices,
    each cut into 8 wedges
Twenty-four ¾-inch squares red bell
    pepper (1 medium pepper)
1 tablespoon chopped fresh parsley
    for garnish (optional)

MAKES 24 SKEWERS

❋ Soak twenty-four 6-inch wooden skewers in water for 30 minutes and drain before using. To marinate the swordfish: Combine the cumin, coriander, paprika, kosher salt, and vegetable oil in a medium bowl. Add the fish and toss to coat until the spices are evenly distributed. Let marinate for at least 15 minutes.

❋ Preheat a grill to medium high or the oven to 400°F. To make the lemon drizzle: Combine the lemon juice, harissa, garlic, kosher salt, and sugar in a small bowl. Slowly whisk in the olive oil. Set aside.

❋ TO ASSEMBLE: Thread a lemon wedge, followed by a piece of swordfish and a piece of red pepper (skin-side first), onto a skewer. Repeat the process until all the ingredients have been used. Place the skewers on a grill rack. Cook, uncovered, for 6 to 8 minutes, or until the fish is opaque throughout, rotating the skewers frequently. If using an oven, place the skewers on a baking sheet lined with aluminum foil in the center of the oven and bake for 5 to 7 minutes. Serve the skewers drizzled with the vinaigrette. Sprinkle with parsley, if desired.

DO-AHEAD TIPS: The drizzle can be made 1 day in advance and refrigerated. Serve at room temperature. The skewers can be cooked up to 1 day in advance. To reheat, place the skewers on a baking sheet lined with aluminum foil and cover with more foil. Bake in a preheated 350°F oven for 5 minutes, or until heated through, and serve as directed.

Mushrooms and Sweet Pearl Onions with Cabernet Syrup

Something about the deep purple color of these onions makes us want to serve them for the holidays. Their rich color and hearty flavor remind us of the incredibly decadent boeuf bourguignon Mom made for special family gatherings in the dead of winter. We're convinced that even natives of Burgundy would approve of these majestic jewels.

24 white or cremini mushrooms
   (about 1½-inch caps), stemmed
¼ cup olive oil or bacon fat
¼ teaspoon kosher salt
⅛ teaspoon ground pepper

PEARL ONIONS WITH CABERNET
   SYRUP:
1¼ cups full-bodied red wine, such as
   Cabernet
1¼ teaspoons sugar
¼ teaspoon kosher salt
⅛ teaspoon ground pepper
1 bay leaf
24 pearl onions, peeled and trimmed
   (see note)
1 tablespoon salted butter
1 tablespoon chopped fresh thyme
Thyme flowers or chopped fresh
   chives or parsley for garnish

MAKES 24 SKEWERS

※ Preheat the oven to 350°F. Line a baking sheet with aluminum foil. Put the mushrooms in a small bowl and toss with olive oil or bacon fat, kosher salt, and pepper. Spread evenly on the prepared pan, stem-side up, and cook for 30 minutes, or until tender and crispy brown. Turn the mushrooms after about 20 minutes and continue cooking them face down.

※ TO MAKE THE ONIONS: Combine the wine, sugar, kosher salt, pepper, and bay leaf in a small non-reactive saucepan. Add the onions and bring to a boil over high heat. Cook, swirling frequently, until the wine is reduced to syrup consistency and the onions are tender, 12 to 15 minutes. Remove from heat. Add the butter and thyme, and stir until the butter has melted. Transfer the onions to a plate and let cool to the touch.

※ TO ASSEMBLE: Place 1 onion inside each mushroom and skewer them with a toothpick. Brush the mushrooms with any remaining glaze. Garnish with the thyme flowers or herbs and serve immediately.

DO-AHEAD TIPS: This dish can be made 1 day in advance. Reheat, covered with aluminum foil, in a preheated 350°F oven for about 10 minutes. Garnish just before serving.

NOTE: *Peeling pearl onions can be made easier buy soaking them in water for 15 minutes to loosen their skins.*

Apple Wood–Smoked Bacon-Wrapped Scallops with Tamari Glaze

Smoky bacon embraces succulent sea scallops in this heavenly creation, and rosemary and teriyaki provide an earthy dimension. We use tamari in the glaze because we like its distinctively mellow flavor. Tamari resembles soy sauce, but is thicker and less salty, with a more complex flavor profile. If you can't find the rosemary sprigs, use 24 toothpicks, soaked in water for 30 minutes, then drained.

TAMARI GLAZE:

2 tablespoons reduced-sodium
    tamari sauce
2 tablespoons maple syrup
1 teaspoon fresh lime juice

8 strips apple wood–smoked bacon,
    stacked and cut into 3- to 4-inch
    pieces (see note)
24 medium sea scallops (about
    1 pound), or 12 large sea scallops,
    cut in half vertically
1 heaping tablespoon fresh rosemary
    leaves
Freshly ground pepper to taste
24 sturdy 3-inch rosemary sprigs
    (strip the leaves from the bot-
    tom inch of each sprig)

MAKES 24 SKEWERS

✽ TO MAKE THE TAMARI GLAZE: Combine the tamari, maple syrup, and lime juice in a small saucepan. Boil over medium heat, whisking frequently, until thick, syrupy, and reduced by half, 5 to 7 minutes. Keep a very close eye on this, to avoid burning. Remove from heat.

✽ TO ASSEMBLE: Preheat the broiler. Line a baking sheet with aluminum foil. Lay several pieces of bacon at a time, vertically, on a work surface. Place a scallop flat-side down on the base of each bacon strip and place 3 or 4 rosemary leaves on top of each scallop. Wrap with the bacon and place seam-side down on the prepared pan. Repeat the process until all of the scallops have been wrapped. Liberally season each bacon-wrapped scallop with pepper.

✽ Broil the scallops about 5 inches from the heat source until the bacon is partially crisp and brown around the edges, 10 to 15 minutes. (Keep a close eye on the scallops to avoid burning the bacon, as each oven cooks differently.) Remove from the oven and let cool slightly. Brush the scallops with tamari glaze and skewer each one, from the top, with a rosemary sprig. Serve hot.

DO-AHEAD TIPS: The scallops can be wrapped with bacon and refrigerated, uncooked, up to 1 day in advance. Cook and serve as directed.

NOTE: *The bacon should be cut according to the size of the scallops. It should barely overlap each scallop or scallop half. Try wrapping 1 strip of bacon around a scallop to measure the correct length of bacon (about 3 to 4 inches) before cutting all the bacon strips.*

Preparing this tropical sensation can get a little messy, but the extra effort in the kitchen will be well rewarded. For an understated, elegant touch, serve these cocktail sticks on a glass platter covered with thinly sliced limes. Macadamia nuts give the dish its rich, tropical flair, but peanuts and cashews make delicious, economical alternatives.

Twenty-four 1-inch cubes boneless,
  skinless chicken breast (about
  12 ounces)
½ teaspoon kosher salt
½ teaspoon curry powder
1 tablespoon vegetable oil
¾ cup mango chutney, preferably
  Major Grey's
1 cup macadamia nuts, finely
  chopped by hand (see note)
¼ cup chopped fresh cilantro

MAKES 24 SKEWERS

NOTE: *For best results, use a very sharp knife to chop the nuts. Resist the temptation to use the food processor to chop the nuts, because too much moisture will be released.*

❀ Soak twenty-four 6-inch wooden skewers in water for 30 minutes, then drain.

❀ Preheat the oven to 350°F.

❀ Toss the chicken with the kosher salt and curry powder in a medium bowl. Heat the oil in a large nonstick skillet over high heat. Add the chicken. Cook until brown and crisp, about 5 minutes, stirring to brown on all sides. Remove the chicken with a slotted spoon and drain on paper towels. Let cool.

❀ TO ASSEMBLE: Put the chutney in a bowl and add the chicken. Toss gently. Combine the nuts and cilantro in a separate bowl and set half of that mixture aside. Transfer the chicken pieces, in batches, to the bowl with half the nut mixture. Coat the chicken evenly with the nuts and place on a baking sheet. After about half the chicken has been covered with nuts, the nut mixture may be wet and hard to handle. At this point, use the reserved mixture to coat the remaining chicken. Thread 1 piece of chicken onto each skewer.

❀ Place the skewers on a baking sheet and cover loosely with aluminum foil. Bake until warm, about 5 minutes. Serve immediately. This hors d'oeuvre is also delicious served room temperature or slightly chilled.

DO-AHEAD TIPS: The chicken can be prepared and refrigerated up to 1 day in advance. To serve warm, heat as directed.

Balsamic Sun-Dried Tomatoes, Broccoli, and Smoked Gouda

We love the simplicity of this hors d'oeuvre. If you aren't a lover of smoked Gouda, substitute an herbed jack, a sharp Wisconsin Cheddar, or even a firm Brie. To take this recipe one step further, toss the broccoli with basil pesto. And, for a stunning presentation, buy an extra head of broccoli, slice off its stem, and place it in the center of a serving dish, using the broccoli as a base to hold the skewers upright.

Twenty-four 1-inch broccoli florets, steamed (see note)

2 tablespoons high-quality extra-virgin olive oil

Kosher salt and freshly ground pepper to taste

24 whole oil-packed sun-dried tomatoes, drained

2 teaspoons high-quality balsamic vinegar

Twenty-four ½-inch pieces smoked Gouda (about 4 ounces, rinds removed)

MAKES 24 SKEWERS

❋ Choose twenty-four 6-inch wooden or decorative skewers. If using wooden skewers, soak them in water for 30 minutes, then drain.

❋ Toss the broccoli florets with the olive oil in a small bowl. Season with kosher salt and pepper. In a separate bowl, lightly toss the sun-dried tomatoes and balsamic vinegar. Season with pepper.

❋ TO ASSEMBLE: Thread a broccoli floret, then a sun-dried tomato (folded in half) and a piece of smoked Gouda, onto a skewer. Repeat the process until all ingredients have been used. Serve at room temperature.

DO-AHEAD TIPS: The skewers can be assembled 1 day in advance and refrigerated. Remove from the refrigerator about 15 minutes before serving.

NOTE: *Steam broccoli florets until bright green and tender, about 3 minutes. Plunge into salted ice water (we use 8 cups water and 2 teaspoons kosher salt).*

Lamb with Mint-Mustard Dipping Sauce

*These skewers inspire gluttony! The dip-
ping sauce is so versatile, we always whip
up a double batch to pair with chicken,
salmon, pork, or pasta later in the week.
Fresh rosemary sprig skewers create a
dramatic presentation, and the rosemary
also infuses the lamb with subtle herbal
flavor. Don't sweat it, though, if you
can't find sturdy sprigs of rosemary;
toothpicks can be used instead.*

DIPPING SAUCE:

3 tablespoons whole-grain mustard

2 tablespoons champagne vinegar

1½ teaspoons honey

1 small garlic clove, smashed

½ teaspoon kosher salt

⅛ teaspoon ground pepper

¾ cup olive oil

¼ cup firmly packed fresh mint
    leaves, coarsely chopped

1 tablespoon olive oil

12 ounces boneless lamb loin,
    trimmed and halved lengthwise

¼ teaspoon kosher salt

⅛ teaspoon ground pepper

24 sturdy rosemary sprigs, about
    4 inches in length (strip the
    leaves from the bottom inch
    of each rosemary sprig)

MAKES ABOUT 24 SKEWERS

✺ TO MAKE THE DIPPING SAUCE:
Combine the mustard, vinegar,
honey, garlic, kosher salt, and pepper
in a blender. Blend until well incorporated. Slowly pour in the olive oil
while the blender is running on low
speed. Blend until the oil is emulsi-
fied. Add the mint and pulse. Set
aside.

✺ Heat the oil in a large skillet over
high heat. Season the lamb with the
kosher salt and pepper. Sear the
lamb until evenly brown, about 3
minutes on each side for medium
rare. Transfer the lamb to a cutting
board, cover loosely with aluminum
foil, and let rest for 10 minutes.

✺ TO ASSEMBLE: Thinly slice the
lamb into ⅛-inch slices. Fold a lamb
slice to create a ribbon effect and
slide onto the base of a rosemary
sprig. Repeat the process until all the
ingredients have been used. Serve
immediately.

DO-AHEAD TIPS: The sauce can be
made and refrigerated 3 to 5 days in
advance. It is best served at room temperature. The lamb can be seared,
sliced, and skewered up to 8 hours in
advance and refrigerated. To reheat,
place the lamb skewers on a baking
sheet lined with aluminum foil and
cover with more foil. Bake in a preheated 350°F oven until slightly warm,
3 to 5 minutes.

The ballots are in! After preparing this Mediterranean-inspired roll-up using mint, arugula, and basil, our friends unanimously cast their votes in favor of mint. The herb's crisp, cool character enlivens the rustic combination of eggplant and chèvre. We'd be hard-pressed to pick a favorite recipe in this book, but this is right up at the top. For best results, use a well-sharpened knife or mandoline to slice the eggplant.

3 tablespoons balsamic vinegar

3 tablespoons olive oil

⅛ teaspoon ground pepper

Twenty-four ⅛-inch-thick lengthwise slices Japanese eggplant (about five 3-ounce eggplants)

¾ teaspoon kosher salt

¼ cup chèvre (fresh goat cheese)

24 medium to large fresh mint leaves

One 4-ounce jar pimientos, drained

MAKES 24 ROLLS

❄ Preheat a grill to medium high or the oven to 400°F.

❄ Combine the vinegar, olive oil, and pepper in a small bowl. Remove and reserve half. Place the eggplant on a baking sheet and brush both sides with half the remaining vinaigrette. Season with the kosher salt. Transfer to the grill and cook until tender, turning occasionally, about 4 minutes per side. Or, place the baking sheet in the oven and cook until tender, about 10 minutes. Brush with the reserved vinaigrette and refrigerate until chilled.

❄ Place the eggplant slices vertically on a work surface. Trim them to 3-by-1½-inch strips. Place about ½ teaspoon chèvre on one end of each eggplant slice; top with a mint leaf, allowing it to extend beyond the sides of the eggplant. Roll the eggplant up and place on the work surface, seam-side down. Place a piece of pimiento on top and secure with a toothpick. (Press the toothpick all the way through the opposite end.) Repeat the process until all the ingredients have been used. Serve.

DO-AHEAD TIPS: The eggplant can be prepared up to 3 days in advance. The eggplant rolls can be assembled and refrigerated up to 4 hours in advance. Remove from the refrigerator about 15 minutes before serving.

Nothing beats the clean, crisp flavor combination of mint and cucumber. Served cold, these soothing skewers are perfect for pool-party noshing. Paired with a fruit-forward Chardonnay or a lively white sangria, they elevate sunbathing to luxurious new heights.

DIPPING SAUCE:

1½ cups coarsely chopped ripe
    mango
¼ cup fresh orange juice
2 teaspoons fresh lime juice
¼ teaspoon kosher salt
3 tablespoons chopped green onion,
    green part only
2 tablespoons chopped fresh basil
1½ teaspoons minced green jalapeño

4 cups water
1½ teaspoons kosher salt
Twenty-four ¾-inch cubes boneless,
    skinless chicken breast (about
    ¾ pound)
1 English cucumber, seeded, quar-
    tered, and cut into twenty-four
    ¼-inch slices
24 small to medium fresh mint
    leaves

MAKES 24 SKEWERS

✸ Choose twenty-four 6-inch wooden or decorative skewers. If using wooden skewers, soak them in water for 30 minutes, then drain.

✸ TO MAKE THE DIPPING SAUCE: Put the mango, orange juice, lime juice, and kosher salt in a blender and process until well blended. Pour into a small bowl and add the green onion, basil, and jalapeño. Mix well. Refrigerate until chilled. Season to taste with more lime juice and salt, if necessary.

✸ Place the water in a medium saucepan over medium-high heat and bring to a boil. Season with kosher salt and add the chicken. Simmer until cooked through, 3 to 5 minutes. Transfer the chicken to paper towels to drain. Let cool.

✸ TO ASSEMBLE: Thread a piece of cucumber through the flesh (peel side facing out) onto a skewer, followed by a mint leaf and a piece of chicken. Set the skewer on a plate so that the peel of the cucumber faces upward. Repeat until all of the ingredients have been used. Refrigerate until chilled. Serve with the mango dipping sauce.

DO-AHEAD TIPS: The dipping sauce can be prepared up to 1 day in advance (it will thicken; add orange juice until it reaches a desired consistency). Assemble the skewers up to 1 day in advance. Cover with a damp towel, followed by plastic wrap.

Glazed Shrimp with Bourbon Barbecue Dunk

This tantalizing barbecue-sauce blend is out of this world! Double the recipe to have extra on hand. In a matter of seconds, it turns ordinary pork tenderloin, chicken breast, or brisket into a world-class feast. Our secret? Bottled chili sauce. Although its name suggests high spice, this mild condiment resembles a slightly piquant ketchup with considerably less sweetness. Look for it in the condiment section of your supermarket.

DUNK:

1¼ cups chili sauce

¼ cup finely chopped green onions

¼ cup olive oil

2 tablespoons molasses

2 tablespoons bourbon

2 tablespoons Worcestershire sauce

2 tablespoons low-sodium soy sauce

1 teaspoon Tabasco sauce

2 teaspoons minced garlic

24 medium shrimp, peeled and deveined (about 1 pound)

MAKES 24 SKEWERS

✻ TO MAKE THE DUNK: Whisk together the chili sauce, green onions, olive oil, molasses, bourbon, Worcestershire sauce, soy sauce, Tabasco, and garlic in a small bowl. Reserve 1 cup for a dipping sauce and refrigerate. Place the shrimp and the remaining dunk in a large self-sealing plastic bag. Seal the bag and shake to coat. Marinate in the refrigerator for at least 15 minutes or up to 8 hours.

✻ Soak twenty-four 6-inch wooden skewers in water for 30 minutes; drain before using. Preheat a grill to medium high or the oven to 450°F.

✻ TO ASSEMBLE: Drain the shrimp. Thread 1 shrimp onto each skewer. If using a grill, brush or spray the grill rack with oil. Place the skewers on the grill rack and grill, uncovered, for about 5 minutes, rotating the skewers frequently until the shrimp are pink. If using the oven, place the skewers on a baking sheet lined with aluminum foil and cover loosely with more foil. Bake for 5 to 7 minutes. Serve warm, at room temperature, or chilled, with the reserved dunk.

DO-AHEAD TIPS: The dunk can be made 3 to 5 days in advance. The shrimp can be marinated, skewered, and cooked 1 day in advance. To reheat, place the skewers on a baking sheet lined with aluminum foil and cover loosely with more foil. Bake in a preheated 350°F oven for 5 minutes, or until warm.

Lobster and Asparagus with Lemony Tarragon Aioli

Two culinary gems—lobster and asparagus—meld luxuriously in this recipe under a voluptuous cloak of mayonnaise perfumed with citrus and herbs. If you're shy on funds, frozen lobster tails will do the trick, as will monkfish with its dense, buttery flesh. (Cut monkfish into 1-inch pieces before cooking.) The aioli is at its best when made at least 1 day in advance and served at room temperature.

LEMONY TARRAGON AIOLI:

1 cup mayonnaise

1 tablespoon chopped fresh parsley

1 tablespoon minced shallots

1 tablespoon fresh lemon juice

1 teaspoon grated lemon zest

2 teaspoons minced garlic

½ teaspoon dried tarragon

Freshly ground pepper to taste

2 tablespoons water, if needed

1 tablespoon kosher salt

Two 8-ounce lobster tails (thawed, if frozen)

36 medium asparagus tips (about 1½ inches long)

MAKES 36 SKEWERS

✳ TO MAKE THE AIOLI: Whisk together the mayonnaise, parsley, shallots, lemon juice, lemon zest, garlic, tarragon, and pepper in a small bowl. Adjust the consistency by adding 2 tablespoons water, if necessary. The dipping sauce should be looser than the average mayonnaise consistency. Refrigerate for at least 30 minutes so the flavors will marry.

✳ Choose thirty-six 6-inch wooden or decorative skewers. If using wooden skewers, soak them in water for 30 minutes; drain.

✳ Bring a 4-quart pot of water to a boil and add the kosher salt. Plunge the lobster tails into the boiling water, reduce heat to a simmer, and cook for 10 minutes. Drain and plunge the lobster tails into salted ice water (we use 8 cups water and 2 teaspoons kosher salt) for about 5 minutes to stop the cooking. To remove the lobster meat from the tails, use kitchen shears to cut a lengthwise slit on each side of the underside of each shell. Remove the meat and cut it into thirty-six 1-inch pieces. Blanch the asparagus in salted boiling water until tender, yet crisp, about 3 minutes. Refresh in salted ice water and drain.

✳ TO ASSEMBLE: Thread 1 asparagus tip onto each skewer, followed by 1 piece of lobster. Repeat until all of the ingredients have been used. Serve chilled, with the aioli.

DO-AHEAD TIPS: The aioli can be made 3 days in advance. The skewers can be prepared 1 day in advance and refrigerated.

Beef Satay

When typically skewered in long, narrow strips, this traditional Thai appetizer needs a knife and fork. For passing at a cocktail party, we have found that bunching the meat tightly at the end of the skewer turns this into a finger food. Satay looks its best when served cradled in the center of a bright Boston lettuce leaf or stacked atop a colorful bed of shaved red cabbage. Try substituting chicken or pork for the beef in this recipe. And if you're counting calories, light coconut milk also works beautifully.

MAKES 36 SKEWERS

MARINADE:

¼ cup peanut oil

4 medium garlic cloves, thinly sliced

Thirty-six 1½-by-2½-by-¼-inch slices flank steak or tenderloin (about 12 ounces)

PEANUT SAUCE:

1½ cups coconut milk

1 tablespoon plus 2 teaspoons packed brown sugar

1 tablespoon fish sauce

¾ teaspoon green curry paste

¼ cup crunchy peanut butter

1 tablespoon fresh lime juice

¼ teaspoon kosher salt

⅛ teaspoon ground pepper

1 tablespoon chopped fresh cilantro (optional)

✳ TO MAKE THE MARINADE: Combine the oil and the garlic in a small bowl; add the meat, stir until the oil is evenly distributed, and cover the meat with plastic wrap. Refrigerate for at least 30 minutes. Meanwhile, soak thirty-six 6-inch wooden skewers in water for 30 minutes; drain before using.

✳ TO MAKE THE PEANUT SAUCE: Combine the coconut milk, brown sugar, fish sauce, and green curry paste in a medium nonreactive saucepan. Bring the mixture to a boil. Reduce heat and simmer for 15 to 20 minutes, stirring frequently with a whisk. The mixture will begin to thicken. Remove from heat. Whisk in the peanut butter and lime juice. Set aside for at least 30 minutes; the mixture will thicken as it cools.

✳ TO ASSEMBLE: Preheat a grill to medium high or the oven to 450°F. Season the beef with salt and pepper, stirring to coat evenly. Weave 1 strip of meat lengthwise onto each skewer, creating a tightly stacked ribbon effect. Discard any garlic that may have stuck to the meat. Grill, uncovered, for about 5 minutes, rotating the skewers frequently, until the meat is pink in the center, or cooked to the desired doneness. Or, place the skewers on a baking sheet lined with aluminum foil and bake for 8 to 10 minutes. Remove from grill or oven. Serve hot or at room temperature, with warm or room temperature peanut sauce. Garnish with cilantro before serving, if desired.

DO-AHEAD TIPS: The peanut sauce can be made 3 days in advance and refrigerated. The beef can be marinated 2 days in advance; it can be cooked 1 day in advance and refrigerated. Reheat in a preheated 350°F oven, covered with aluminum foil, for about 5 minutes.

Smoked Turkey, Avocado, and Bacon with Blue Cheese Vinaigrette

Even Bob Cobb would approve of this hip variation on his timeless salad of the 1920s. Long live the spectacular combination of turkey, bacon, and avocado drenched in a tangy blue cheese vinaigrette. We've piled the key ingredients of Cobb's salad on a stick and transformed it into a seductive finger food. For best results, purchase a high-quality blue cheese, and artfully arrange these colorful skewers on a bed of Boston lettuce sprinkled with fresh corn kernels. For a shortcut, purchase a bottle of your favorite blue cheese dressing (ranch dressing is yummy too).

VINAIGRETTE:

2 tablespoons red wine vinegar

¼ cup water

¾ teaspoon sugar

⅛ teaspoon ground pepper

½ cup olive oil

½ cup crumbled blue cheese, such as Maytag

Kosher salt to taste

4 strips bacon, cut into six ½-inch pieces (stack the strips and cut all at once)

12 ounces thinly sliced (⅛-inch-thick) smoked turkey, cut into twenty-four 1-by-6-inch strips

1 avocado, peeled, pitted, cut into twenty-four ½-inch pieces, and sprinkled with fresh lime juice

MAKES 24 SKEWERS

❋ TO MAKE THE VINAIGRETTE: Process the vinegar, water, sugar, and pepper in a blender until smooth. While the machine is running, add the olive oil in a slow, steady stream. Add the blue cheese and pulse until well incorporated. Add kosher salt, if necessary. Refrigerate until ready to use.

❋ Choose twenty-four 6-inch wooden or decorative skewers. If using wooden skewers, soak them in water for 30 minutes and drain before using. Preheat the oven to 350°F. Line a baking sheet with aluminum foil. Space the bacon pieces evenly on the pan and bake until lightly brown and crisp, 12 to 15 minutes. Remove from the oven and transfer the bacon to paper towels to drain. Let cool.

❋ TO ASSEMBLE: Lay several strips of turkey, vertically, on a work surface. Place a piece of avocado and bacon at the base of each turkey strip and roll tightly, securing with a skewer. Repeat the process until all of the ingredients are used. Serve with a small bowl of the blue cheese vinaigrette.

DO-AHEAD TIPS: The vinaigrette can be made up to 5 days in advance. The skewers can be assembled and refrigerated up to 8 hours in advance.

Peppery Bacon-Wrapped Watermelon Rind Pickles

We follow one rule of thumb when doling out platter after platter of these divine little numbers: We never mention the watermelon rind pickles, because we anticipate that most guests will shy away. Fellow Southerners share our enthusiasm for these tangy wonders, but entertaining in San Francisco has taught us that not everyone knows about these Southern secrets. To entice guests from beyond the Mason-Dixon line, we present these saying, "Don't ask—just enjoy!" We consistently get rave reviews.

24 watermelon rind pickles, drained
    and cut into uniform bite-sized
    pieces (1 by 1 by ¼ inch is ideal)
2 tablespoons apple cider vinegar
8 strips bacon, stacked and cut into
    3-inch pieces
Freshly ground pepper to taste
Twenty-four diagonally cut 1-inch-
    long green onion slices (green
    parts only)

MAKES 24 SKEWERS

❋ Preheat the oven to 400°F. Line a baking sheet with aluminum foil. Toss the pickles in a bowl with the apple cider vinegar.

❋ TO ASSEMBLE: Lay several pieces of bacon at a time, vertically, on a work surface. Place a pickle on the base of each bacon strip, wrap, and place seam-side down on the prepared pan; the bacon should barely overlap. Repeat the process until all of the pickles have been wrapped. Liberally sprinkle each bacon-wrapped pickle with pepper. Bake until the bacon is partially crisp and brown around the edges, about 15 minutes. Place a fresh green onion slice on each morsel, skewer with a toothpick, and serve immediately.

DO-AHEAD TIPS: The pickles can be wrapped with bacon, cooked, and refrigerated up to 1 day in advance. Reheat in a preheated 350°F oven until warm, 5 to 7 minutes. Skewer and garnish as directed.

Potatoes take the stage as the key ingredient in this recipe, although crusty French bread, broccoli florets, and cooked baby artichoke hearts also make wonderful companions to this cheesy concoction. Go easy on the potatoes. If overcooked, they will fall off the skewer. Although a fancy fondue set is nice for this dish, it isn't essential. Simply serve the cheese in a decorative bowl and pass it while warm, then zap it in the microwave when it gets too cool.

FONDUE:

2 teaspoons olive oil

⅓ cup finely chopped onion

Kosher salt and freshly ground pepper to taste

2 tablespoons dry sherry

½ cup plus 1 tablespoon heavy cream

½ cup (4 ounces) cream cheese at room temperature

½ cup grated Parmesan cheese

⅓ cup shredded Gruyère cheese

1 teaspoon fresh lemon juice

⅛ teaspoon ground nutmeg

Twenty-four 1-inch pieces red potatoes (about 12 ounces)

1 tablespoon extra-virgin olive oil

1 tablespoon minced fresh parsley

1 tablespoon chopped fresh chives for garnish

MAKES 24 SKEWERS

DO-AHEAD TIPS: The potatoes can be boiled, then tossed in oil, 4 to 6 hours before serving. (Cooked potatoes are best when not refrigerated.) Warm slightly in a preheated 350°F oven, covered with aluminum foil, or in a microwave, covered with plastic wrap. Garnish as directed. The cheese mixture can be made up to 2 days in advance and heated slowly over low heat, or reheated in the microwave. Serve as directed.

❈ If you don't have fondue forks, choose twenty-four 6-inch wooden skewers and soak them in water for 30 minutes; drain before using.

❈ TO MAKE THE FONDUE: Put the olive oil in a medium, heavy saucepan. Place over medium heat and add the onions. Season with kosher salt and pepper. Cook until the onions are tender, 3 to 5 minutes. Add the sherry and cook until liquid is nearly evaporated, about 1 minute. Reduce heat to low and add the cream, cream cheese, Parmesan, and Gruyère. Whisk together frequently until the cheese is melted and the mixture is well incorporated. Add the lemon juice and nutmeg and season with pepper and more kosher salt, if necessary. Remove from heat, cover, and keep warm.

❈ Place the potatoes in a medium saucepan and add salted water to cover. (We use about 6 cups water and 2 teaspoons kosher salt.) Bring to a boil over high heat and reduce heat to a simmer. Cook until the potatoes are barely tender when pierced with a knife, about 8 minutes. Remove from heat, drain, and spread on a plate. Brush with olive oil and sprinkle with parsley.

❈ TO ASSEMBLE: Spear each potato with a skewer, sprinkle the warm cheese sauce with the chives, and serve immediately, with the skewers.

Spicy Tofu with Cilantro and Smoky Black Bean Dip

One taste of this hors d'oeuvre, and even the most strident tofu skeptic will be converted. The tofu in this recipe doesn't have to be cooked, making this skewer perfect for those times when you're in need of an appetizer in a jiff. Simply marinate it and serve with the dipping sauce for a wonderful variation. If you have leftover bean dip, slather it on a chicken breast with a dab of salsa and sour cream. Fans of fire take note: We've called for a conservative amount of chipotle chiles in the recipe, as their heat becomes more pronounced over time. Up the chile ante at your own risk!

MARINADE:

2 tablespoons olive oil

¼ teaspoon minced canned chipotle
    chile in adobo sauce

½ teaspoon minced garlic

¼ teaspoon kosher salt

Thirty ¾-inch cubes firm tofu
    (8 ounces)

SMOKY BLACK BEAN DIP:

One 15-ounce can black beans,
    drained (liquid reserved)

1 tablespoon ketchup

1 teaspoon ground cumin

1 teaspoon ground coriander

½ teaspoon minced canned
    chipotle chile in adobo sauce

½ teaspoon minced garlic

1 teaspoon fresh lime juice

Kosher salt to taste

30 fresh cilantro leaves for garnish

MAKES 30 SKEWERS

❄ TO MARINATE THE TOFU:
Combine the olive oil, chile, garlic, and kosher salt in a small bowl. Add the tofu and toss gently to coat. Marinate for about 15 minutes.

❄ Preheat the oven to 375°F. Line a baking sheet with aluminum foil.

❄ TO MAKE THE SMOKY BLACK BEAN DIP: Combine the black beans, ½ cup of reserved bean broth, ketchup, cumin, coriander, chile, garlic, and lime juice in a food processor. Process until well incorporated but not completely smooth, about 5 seconds. Season with kosher salt, if necessary. Set aside.

❄ Place the marinated tofu on the prepared pan and bake until lightly browned, 15 to 20 minutes.

❄ TO ASSEMBLE: Place a cilantro leaf on top of each cube of tofu and skewer together with a toothpick or decorative skewer. Serve hot, with the bean dip.

DO-AHEAD TIPS: The bean dip can be made 2 days in advance and refrigerated. Remove from the refrigerator at least 30 minutes before serving. The tofu can be marinated and refrigerated, uncooked, up to 1 day in advance. Cook and serve as directed.

Tuna with Black Olives and Marinated Artichoke Crowns

Marinated artichoke crowns (baby artichoke hearts with no leaves attached) have hit our list of favorite prepared products. They work extremely well in this dish, although the more familiar, easier-to-find, marinated artichoke hearts will suffice. If you select artichoke hearts, keep in mind that they vary in shape and size and may have tough outer leaves. Cut away the leaves as needed for artichokes that are the right size for hors d'oeuvres. We save our extra leaves for use as an unexpected flourish in salads.

Twenty-four 1-by-1-by-½-inch pieces
    ahi tuna (about 8 ounces)
2 teaspoons olive oil
¼ teaspoon kosher salt
⅛ teaspoon ground pepper
1½ teaspoons dried oregano
1 tablespoon chopped fresh parsley
12 marinated artichoke crowns,
    drained and halved
    (one 8-ounce jar)
12 kalamata olives, pitted and
    halved lengthwise

MAKES 24 SKEWERS

✳ Soak twenty-four 6-inch wooden skewers in water for 30 minutes, then drain. Or, select 24 decorative skewers. Heat a grill pan over medium-high heat or preheat a grill to medium high (see note).

✳ Toss the tuna in a bowl with the olive oil, kosher salt, and pepper. Place the tuna on the grill pan or grill rack and cook until the exterior begins to brown slightly but the center is still pink, about 3 minutes, turning at least once. (If the tuna adheres to the grill, a spatula comes in handy.) Transfer the tuna to a bowl and toss with the oregano.

✳ TO ASSEMBLE: Sprinkle 2 teaspoons of the parsley over the tuna. In a separate bowl, gently toss the artichokes with the remaining parsley. Thread 1 black olive half onto each skewer, followed by a piece of tuna and a piece of artichoke. Repeat until all of the ingredients have been used. This dish is best when the tuna is hot and the olives and artichokes are chilled, but it is also delicious when all the components are at room temperature or cold.

DO-AHEAD TIPS: The skewers can be assembled and cooked 1 day in advance and refrigerated. In this case, brush the skewers with a high-quality extra virgin olive oil just before serving.

NOTE: Our favorite way to cook the tuna for this dish is in a grill pan, because you get the grill marks and delicious flavor without having to worry about the tuna falling through the grill rack onto the coals.

Spinach Tortellini with Roasted Red Pepper Pesto

Nothing is easier than skewering pasta for quick entertaining. The host of available styles, shapes, flavors, and sizes encourages creativity. When assembling your skewers, try alternating pastas by color or flavor, then top off the skewer with an olive, a sun-dried tomato, or a small cherry tomato for an edible adornment.

ROASTED RED PEPPER PESTO:

1 cup roasted red peppers
  (see page 21)
½ cup firmly packed fresh parsley
  leaves
½ cup pine nuts, toasted
3 tablespoons olive oil
1 tablespoon tomato paste
1 tablespoon balsamic vinegar
1 teaspoon minced garlic
½ teaspoon herbes de Provence
¼ teaspoon kosher salt
⅛ teaspoon ground pepper

24 cheese-filled spinach tortellini,
  preferably fresh (about 6 ounces)
2 teaspoons extra-virgin olive oil
Kosher salt and freshly ground
  pepper to taste

MAKES 24 SKEWERS

✽ Select twenty-four 6-inch wooden or decorative skewers. If using wooden ones, soak them in water for 30 minutes, then drain.

✽ TO MAKE THE PESTO: Combine the red peppers, parsley leaves, pine nuts, olive oil, tomato paste, balsamic vinegar, garlic, herbes de Provence, kosher salt, and pepper in a food processor. Blend until smooth. Set aside.

✽ Bring a medium pot of salted water to a boil (we use about 8 cups water and 2 teaspoons kosher salt). Cook the pasta according to directions on the package, or about 6 to 8 minutes for fresh pasta, and 12 to 15 minutes for dried, but taste along the way. The final result should be al dente, or slightly firm to the bite. Be careful not to overcook. Drain and toss with extra-virgin olive oil, salt, and pepper. Thread a piece of pasta on each skewer and serve along side a bowl of pesto. Both are delicious served either hot or at room temperature.

DO-AHEAD TIPS: The sauce can be made 2 days in advance and served as directed. The pasta can be cooked and skewered about 3 hours in advance and covered tightly with plastic wrap. Do not refrigerate the pasta before serving.

Seekers of harmony will appreciate this intensely perfumed pork pick infused with Chinese five-spice powder. Although the components of this aromatic spice mixture vary, the blend traditionally contains cinnamon, star anise, fennel, Szechwan peppercorns, and cloves—flavors the Chinese ancients associated with the five elements necessary for a balanced universe: wood, metal, water, fire, and earth.

1½ teaspoons Chinese five-spice
    powder
¼ teaspoon kosher salt
1 tablespoon vegetable oil
Twenty-four ¾-inch cubes
    trimmed boneless pork loin
    (about 1 pound)
¼ cup hoisin sauce
2 teaspoons Asian sesame oil
24 whole canned water chestnuts,
    drained (one 8-ounce can);
    see note
Twenty-four 1-inch diagonal pieces
    snow peas, blanched
2 teaspoons sesame seeds, lightly
    toasted

MAKES 24 SKEWERS

NOTE: *Canned water chestnuts come in varying sizes, thus the number per 8-ounce can varies immensely. If your can contains about 15 water chestnuts, then they are on the large side and can be cut in half for this recipe.*

✸ Soak twenty-four 6-inch wooden skewers in water for 30 minutes; drain before using. Preheat the oven to 450°F. Line a baking pan with aluminum foil.

✸ Combine the five-spice powder, salt, and vegetable oil in a medium bowl. Add the pork and toss to coat until the spices are evenly distributed. Place the seasoned pork evenly on the prepared pan. Bake until cooked through, 6 to 8 minutes. Let cool.

✸ Whisk the hoisin and sesame oil together in a medium bowl. Toss the cooked pork and the water chestnuts in the mixture.

✸ TO ASSEMBLE: Lower the oven temperature to 350°F. Thread 1 piece of snow pea onto each skewer, followed by 1 piece of pork and a water chestnut. (Be aware that some water chestnuts will split if threaded too far up the skewer. Barely skewer the chestnut.) Place the completed skewers on the same baking pan. Repeat until all of the ingredients have been used. Sprinkle the skewers with sesame seeds. Cover the pan with aluminum foil and bake the skewers until heated through, 3 to 5 minutes. These are also delicious served room temperature.

DO-AHEAD TIPS: The pork can be marinated and cooked up to 1 day in advance. The skewers can be assembled 1 day in advance and refrigerated. To serve hot, bake as directed. If serving at room temperature, remove from the refrigerator and let sit 20 minutes before serving.

Open-Faced Mini Reubens

This much-loved deli classic tops our list of all-time faves; it's a guaranteed crowd-pleaser time and time again. Surround this humble tidbit with a ring of salty potato chips for casual gatherings. Frilly toothpicks are a must!

6 slices cocktail rye bread (2½-inch squares)

3 tablespoons Thousand Island dressing

3 ounces Swiss cheese, cut into twelve 2½-inch squares

2 ounces paper-thin pastrami, cut into 24 stacks

About 6 cornichons or sour gherkins, drained and cut diagonally into ¼-inch-thick slices

MAKES 24 MINI-SANDWICHES

❋ Preheat the oven to 350°F. Line a baking sheet with aluminum foil.

❋ TO ASSEMBLE: Spread each piece of the cocktail rye bread with Thousand Island dressing. Place a square of Swiss cheese on each piece of bread (if the cheese has lots of holes, cover them with additional cheese) followed by another layer of Thousand Island dressing. Cut each square of rye bread in half diagonally, then in quarters, creating 4 triangles per slice of bread. Top each triangle of bread with a small mound of pastrami and place a cornichon or gherkin slice on top. Place the open-faced mini-sandwiches on the prepared pan and bake until the cheese begins to melt, about 5 minutes. Push a decorative toothpick through each sandwich. Serve warm.

DO-AHEAD TIPS: These can be prepared 4 to 6 hours in advance and refrigerated. Heat as directed just before serving.

We love yellow squash and its sister, zuc-chini—but never raw! These treasures of the vegetable world show up on a crudité platter looking cold and anemic. Yet roasted, the sugars in the squashes caramelize, invigorating them with sat-isfying sweetness. Following this recipe, we offer several other suggestions for skewered vegetable combinations. Our hope? To breathe new life into the some-what lackluster "veggie and dip" habit.

GREEN ONION AND BASIL DIP:

¾ cup regular or low-fat mayonnaise
⅓ cup buttermilk
¼ cup coarsely chopped fresh basil
    leaves
3 tablespoons coarsely chopped
    green onions (green parts only)
2 teaspoons champagne vinegar
Kosher salt and freshly ground
    pepper to taste

Thirty ¾-by-¾-inch pieces zucchini
    (about 1 small zucchini); see
    note
Thirty ¾-by-¾-inch pieces yellow
    crookneck squash (about 1
    medium yellow squash); see
    note
1 tablespoon olive oil
¼ teaspoon kosher salt
⅛ teaspoon ground pepper

MAKES 30 SKEWERS

Roasted Yellow Squash and Zucchini with Green Onion and Basil Dip

✺ TO MAKE THE DIP: **Combine** the mayonnaise, buttermilk, basil, green onions, and champagne vine-gar in a blender. Blend until smooth. Refrigerate until chilled. Season with kosher salt and pepper to taste.

✺ Soak thirty 6-inch wooden skew-ers in water for 30 minutes; drain before using. Preheat the oven to 400°F. Line a baking sheet with alu-minum foil. Toss the zucchini and squash in a medium bowl with the olive oil, kosher salt, and pepper.

✺ TO ASSEMBLE: **Thread 1 piece** of zucchini onto each skewer, fol-lowed by 1 piece of squash. It is best to skewer through the flesh (not through the skin), so the colorful skin is visible. Repeat until all ingredients have been used. Place on the baking sheet and cook in the center of the oven until the vegetables are tender, about 15 minutes. Let cool slightly. Serve barely warm or at room tem-perature with the sauce. These are also delicious cold.

DO-AHEAD TIPS: The dip can be made 3 days in advance. The skewers can be cooked and refrigerated 1 day in advance. Serve as directed.

NOTE: *Cut the zucchini and squash as uni-formly as possible, though they will be slightly irregular in size and shape.*

We love the idea of the skewered crudité because it turns the ordinary veggie platter into a masterpiece with very little work. In addition to the visual appeal, we like the layers of flavor and texture that accompany each bite. Feel free to mix and match with other vegetable combinations.

GREEN BEANS AND CARROT DISKS: Cut green beans into 1½-inch pieces. Peel and cut carrots into ¼-inch-thick circles or semi-circles according to the width of the carrot. Blanch the carrots in salted boiling water until barely cooked and crisp, about 1 minute. Refresh in salted ice water and drain. (We use 8 cups water and 2 teaspoons kosher salt for blanching and for refreshing.) Blanch the green beans until barely cooked and crisp, about 3 minutes. Refresh in salted ice water and drain. Thread 2 green bean pieces and 2 carrot pieces, in alternating fashion, on each skewer. Serve with Green Onion and Basil Dip (page 53). These can be assembled and refrigerated up to 1 day in advance.

SNOW PEA DIAMONDS AND RED BELL PEPPER SQUARES: Cut the snow peas diagonally, creating 1-inch diamonds. Cut the red bell pepper into 1-inch squares. Thread 1 piece of snow pea, then a red pepper square, then another snow pea on each skewer. Serve with Green Onion and Basil Dip (page 53). These can be assembled and refrigerated up to 1 day in advance.

BROCCOLI FLORETS AND CHERRY TOMATOES: Blanch bite-sized (1¼-inch) broccoli florets until tender yet crisp, about 1 minute. Refresh in salted ice water and drain. (We use 8 cups water and 2 teaspoons kosher salt for blanching and for refreshing.) Thread 1 broccoli floret followed by a cherry tomato (if large, cut in half) on each skewer. Serve with Green Onion and Basil Dip (page 53). These can be assembled and refrigerated up to 1 day in advance.

ASPARAGUS TIPS AND NEW POTATOES: Blanch asparagus tips (about 1 inch in length) until tender, yet crisp, about 3 minutes. Refresh in salted ice water and drain. (We use 8 cups water and 2 teaspoons kosher salt for blanching and for refreshing.) Cut potatoes into ¾-inch pieces. Cook in salted simmering water until barely tender when pierced with a skewer, about 8 minutes. (Do not overcook). Drain and spread on a plate to cool. Thread an asparagus tip and a potato on each skewer. Serve with Green Onion and Basil Dip (page 53). These can be assembled 4 to 6 hours in advance and are best not refrigerated.

RADISH WHEELS AND CUCUMBER CUBES: Cut radishes into ¼-inch slices. Cut a medium cucumber in half, remove the seeds, and quarter. Cut into ¼-inch slices. Thread a radish slice, then a cucumber slice, then another radish slice on each skewer. Serve with Green Onion and Basil Dip (page 53). These can be assembled and refrigerated up to 1 day in advance.

Kielbasa and Potatoes with Caraway-Honey Mustard

Gone are the days when sausage meant only ground pork in your choice of "spicy" or "mild." Today, the selection is dizzying, with creations running the gamut from turkey and sun-dried tomato to the mysterious Moroccan merguez to the down-home comfort of reduced-fat kielbasa. Use this recipe as a guideline, and feel free to experiment with different types of sausage.

CARAWAY-HONEY MUSTARD:
½ cup honey mustard
1 tablespoon apple cider vinegar
2 teaspoons caraway seeds
¼ teaspoon ground pepper
½ cup olive oil
Kosher salt to taste

Twenty-four 1-inch cubes peeled
    baking potato (about 1 medium
    potato)
1 tablespoon olive oil or bacon fat
¼ teaspoon kosher salt
⅛ teaspoon ground pepper
Twenty-four ½-inch-thick semi-
    circles kielbasa (about 8 ounces)

MAKES 24 SKEWERS

※ Preheat the oven to 450°F.

※ TO MAKE THE CARAWAY-HONEY MUSTARD: Combine the mustard, vinegar, caraway seeds, and pepper in a small bowl. Gradually whisk in the olive oil. Season with salt. Set aside.

※ Soak twenty-four 6-inch wooden skewers or toothpicks in water while cooking the potatoes and sausage; drain before using.

※ Toss the potatoes in a bowl with the olive oil or bacon fat, salt, and pepper. Place in a glass baking dish and bake, turning once, for about 25 minutes, or until the potatoes are tender and lightly browned around the edges. Add the sausage to the dish after about 20 minutes and bake with the potatoes for about 5 minutes, or until heated through. Let cool to the touch.

※ TO ASSEMBLE: Thread 1 piece of potato on each skewer, followed by 1 piece of kielbasa. Repeat until all of the ingredients have been used. Serve warm with mustard sauce.

DO-AHEAD TIPS: The dipping sauce can be prepared up to 1 week in advance. Cook and skewer the potatoes and sausage up to 1 day in advance. Place on a baking pan, cover loosely with aluminum foil, and reheat in a preheated 450°F oven for about 5 minutes.

Sesame-Crusted Salmon with Pineapple-Miso Sauce

Delicately sweet, slightly acidic miso gives this Japanese-inspired dish its character. We prefer red miso, a paste made of soybeans, brown rice, and sea salt, for its rich flavor, dark color, and salty finish. For a change in presentation, pool the dipping sauce on a shallow plate and arrange the fish on top.

PINEAPPLE-MISO SAUCE:

3 tablespoons frozen pineapple
    juice concentrate, thawed
1 tablespoon plus 1 teaspoon red
    miso
2 teaspoons minced fresh ginger
2 tablespoons water
2 tablespoons canola oil
1 tablespoon Asian sesame oil

Twenty-four ¾-inch cubes
    skinless, boneless salmon
    (about 12 ounces)
1 tablespoon vegetable oil
½ teaspoon kosher salt
¼ teaspoon ground pepper
2 teaspoons black sesame seeds
2 teaspoons white sesame seeds

MAKES 24 SKEWERS

✤ TO MAKE THE SAUCE: Combine the pineapple concentrate, miso, ginger, and water in a small bowl. Gradually whisk in the canola oil and sesame oil. Add more miso to taste, if necessary. (Every miso has a different salt concentration.) Set aside.

✤ Preheat the oven to 400°F. Line a baking sheet with aluminum foil.

✤ TO ASSEMBLE: Toss the salmon in a bowl with the vegetable oil, kosher salt, and pepper. In a separate bowl, combine the black and white sesame seeds. Lightly dip one side of each salmon cube into the sesame seeds. Place on the prepared pan, seed-side up. Bake until the fish is barely opaque throughout, about 5 minutes. Skewer with toothpicks (from the side) and transfer to a serving plate. Serve hot with the sauce for dipping.

DO-AHEAD TIPS: The sauce can be made 3 days in advance and heated just before serving. The salmon can be assembled (without the kosher salt) 6 to 8 hours in advance, but we don't recommend cooking this dish ahead and reheating it. Cook as directed and skewer just before serving.

Smoked Duck with Spiced Apricots and Watercress

This recipe, with its assertive repertoire of flavors, evokes hearthside dining on a cold winter's night. We always include this dish on our holiday party menu, because of its sheer decadence. We never remove the flavorful duck fat because it adds such tremendous character, but this spear is still delicious with the fat removed. Make the call based on your audience. If you are not a duck fan, try this recipe with 12 ounces thinly sliced smoked ham cut into 1-by-6-inch strips. You won't be disappointed.

SPICED APRICOTS:

3 tablespoons apricot jam

1 tablespoon frozen orange juice
    concentrate

1 tablespoon plus 2 teaspoons water

1½ teaspoons Grand Marnier

Pinch of ground cinnamon

Pinch of ground allspice

Pinch of kosher salt

12 dried apricot halves, cut in half

24 thin slices smoked duck breast
    (about 5 ounces)

24 watercress leaves

MAKES 24 SKEWERS

❋ TO MAKE THE SPICED APRICOTS: Stir together the apricot jam, orange juice concentrate, water, and Grand Marnier in a small glass bowl or ramekin. Season with the cinnamon, allspice, and kosher salt. Stir in the apricots. Heat in a microwave on high until the apricots are soft and the sauce becomes syrupy, about 1 minute. Or cook in a very small saucepan over medium heat until soft, about 4 minutes.

❋ Preheat the oven to 300°F. Line a baking sheet with aluminum foil.

❋ TO ASSEMBLE: Lay several strips of duck, vertically, on a work surface. Place an apricot piece on the bottom part of each duck slice. Roll each slice tightly and skewer with a toothpick. Repeat until all the ingredients are used. Place the skewers on the prepared pan and bake until barely heated through, about 5 minutes. Brush each skewer with the remaining apricot glaze and garnish with a watercress leaf. Serve immediately. This dish is also delicious served at room temperature.

DO-AHEAD TIPS: The skewers can be assembled up to 1 day in advance and refrigerated. Reheat and serve as directed.

NOTE: *Our favorite smoked duck is produced by Grimaud Farms. Order it by calling Joie de Vivre at 800-648-8854, or by visiting their website at www.frenchselections.com. Or, you can order smoked duck from D'Artagnan by calling 800-327-8246, or by visiting their website at www.dartagnan.com.*

We know that, with all that you do, sometimes you have no time to cook. So, we've designed this collection of "quick assembly" recipes to keep you from kissing entertaining goodbye. Friends, family, and colleagues will marvel at your ability to pull off impromptu cocktail parties and alfresco meals with such unflappable style. With these skewers, you'll never be caught off guard. In mere minutes, stream- lined, sophisticated hors d'oeuvres like our melon strung with prosciutto; our antipasto pick of cherry tomatoes, marinated artichokes, and moz- zarella; or our debonair roulade of smoked salmon, cream cheese, and Martini onions can exit your kitchen. Cooking for a crowd has never been this easy—in most cases, you don't even have to turn on the stove!

Melon, Prosciutto, and Arugula with Lime-Poppy Seed Vinaigrette

Everyone is familiar with the classic marriage of melon and prosciutto—but wait until you taste this sensational vinaigrette. The astringency of the lime offsets the saltiness of the ham and sweetness of the melon, and the addition of arugula provides a spicy kick. The secret to this recipe is a full-flavored melon that is icy cold. Try stacking these hors d'oeuvres in a cantaloupe or honeydew bowl for a jazzy presentation. (Cut the melon in half, remove the seeds, and cut a small slice off the bottom so that it will lie flat on a serving plate.)

LIME-POPPY SEED VINAIGRETTE:

3 tablespoons fresh lime juice

3 tablespoons sugar

½ teaspoon dry mustard

¼ teaspoon kosher salt

½ cup vegetable oil

2 teaspoons poppy seeds

One 1½- to 2-pound melon
　　(cantaloupe, honeydew, or
　　any other varietal)

6 paper-thin slices prosciutto
　　(about 2 ounces), cut into
　　½-by-5-inch strips (see note)

24 small arugula leaves

MAKES 24 SKEWERS

NOTE: The length of the prosciutto depends on the size of the melon. For best results, the prosciutto strips should barely overlap each piece of melon. Try wrapping 1 strip of prosciutto around a slice of melon to measure the appropriate length (about 4 to 5 inches), before cutting all of them into strips.

✻ TO MAKE THE VINAIGRETTE: Mix together the lime juice, sugar, dry mustard, and kosher salt in a blender. Gradually blend in the vegetable oil. Add the poppy seeds and blend until incorporated. Refrigerate until ready to use.

✻ Cut the melon in half lengthwise and reserve one of the halves for another use. Seed the remaining half, then cut into 4 lengthwise wedges. Remove the rind from each wedge and cut the melon into 1¼-inch pieces, 6 pieces per wedge, so that you have a total of 24. (Melons are all different sizes. These directions are based on an average-sized cantaloupe.)

✻ TO ASSEMBLE: Lay several strips of prosciutto, vertically, on a work surface. Place an arugula leaf on top of each strip of meat in the same vertical fashion. Place a melon wedge on the bottom part of each strip of prosciutto and wrap. Secure with a toothpick or decorative skewer. Repeat the process until all the ingredients have been used. Refrigerate until chilled, about 15 minutes, and serve with the vinaigrette.

DO-AHEAD TIPS: The vinaigrette can be prepared 3 days in advance and refrigerated. The skewers can be assembled 4 to 6 hours in advance and refrigerated.

VARIATION: This prosciutto wrap works well with lots of other fruits, such as mangos, figs, pears, and watermelons.

Cream cheese and olive sandwiches topped our list of favorites as children, and we'd be lost without them as adults. Sinfully creamy, with just the right touch of salt, they taste so grown-up with a dry Martini. Stock up your refrigerator! This skewer does wonders for the spontaneous poolside fete, and can't be beat as impromptu cocktail food.

6 ounces cold cream cheese

24 pimiento-stuffed Spanish olives, drained

Twenty-four 1-inch squares red bell pepper (about 1 medium pepper)

24 fresh flat-leaf parsley leaves for garnish

Paprika for garnishing

MAKES 24 SKEWERS

❋ TO ASSEMBLE: Place about 1 teaspoon of cream cheese on your fingertips and flatten it into a round shape about the size of a quarter. Place an olive in the center of the cream cheese and bring the edges of the cream cheese up to envelop the olive. Gently mold the cream cheese around the olive. To create a perfect sphere, place the olive and cream cheese in the palm of your hand and roll, applying gentle pressure, until a perfect sphere is formed. Repeat the process until all the spheres have been made.

❋ Thread 1 cream cheese sphere, then 1 red pepper square (skin-side first), on each toothpick, and place on a serving plate, pepper-side down. Repeat the process until all the cream cheese spheres and red pepper squares have been used. Garnish each skewer with a parsley leaf. (Press the herb on the cream cheese so that it sticks, for an effective presentation.) Refrigerate for at least 15 minutes, or until slightly chilled. Sprinkle with paprika before serving.

DO-AHEAD TIPS: This dish can be assembled and refrigerated 1 day in advance. Let sit at room temperature for at least 15 minutes before serving. Garnish with paprika just before serving.

Curried Pimiento Cheese and Spinach Pinwheels

Most roulade recipes call for the rolls to be refrigerated for several hours before serving. We've devised a shortcut. Skewering the pinwheel alleviates any worries that it might unravel and removes the need for a long stint in the refrigerator. If you are fighting the clock, simply add some curry to your favorite brand of store-bought pimiento cheese and proceed with the pinwheel assembly.

CURRIED PIMIENTO CHEESE:

⅓ cup mayonnaise

½ teaspoon curry powder

½ teaspoon chili powder

2 teaspoons mango chutney

1¼ cups shredded sharp white
    Cheddar cheese

¼ cup finely chopped celery

2 tablespoons finely chopped red
    onion

Five 6-inch flour tortillas (preferably
    spinach- or tomato-flavored)

One 4-ounce jar sliced pimientos,
    drained

1 cup firmly packed baby spinach
    leaves

MAKES ABOUT 35 SKEWERS

✳ TO MAKE THE CURRIED PIMIENTO CHEESE: Stir together the mayonnaise, curry powder, chili powder, and mango chutney in a medium bowl. Add the Cheddar, celery, and red onion and stir until well incorporated. Refrigerate until chilled.

✳ TO ASSEMBLE: Spread 3 tablespoons of the cheese mixture on each tortilla, leaving a 1-inch border. Sprinkle the top of each wrap with one fifth of the pimientos and one fifth of the spinach. Roll each tortilla into a tight roll and place, seam-side down, on a cutting board. Using a serrated knife, cut off the ends of each roll and slice into ¾-inch-thick pieces. Secure each piece with a toothpick and serve.

DO-AHEAD TIPS: The cheese mixture can be made up to 3 days in advance. The tortillas can be rolled 8 hours in advance, wrapped in plastic wrap and refrigerated. Cut 1 to 2 hours before serving and skewer. Serve slightly chilled.

Creating a simpler hors d'oeuvre as delicious as this one would be difficult. If fresh vine-ripened tomatoes are not at their peak, substitute oil-packed sundried tomatoes to capture the fruit's intense flavor. Or, simply forget the tomatoes altogether and relish the velvety-softness of the mozzarella against the nutty fullness of the artichoke.

24 marinated artichoke hearts, drained, trimmed into ¾-inch pieces, and chilled
2 teaspoons chopped fresh parsley
Twenty-four ½-inch pieces mozzarella cheese, preferably fresh bocconcini (about 4 ounces)
1 teaspoon extra-virgin olive oil
⅛ teaspoon ground pepper
Kosher salt to taste, if necessary
24 small cherry tomatoes (or 12 large, halved), preferably Sweet 100's

MAKES 24 SKEWERS

Cherry Tomatoes, Marinated Artichoke Hearts, and Mozzarella

✺ Choose twenty-four 6-inch decorative or wooden skewers; if using wooden ones, soak them in water for 30 minutes, then drain.

✺ Place the artichokes in a bowl and sprinkle with the parsley. Toss very gently. Toss the mozzarella pieces in a separate bowl with the olive oil and pepper. Season with kosher salt, if necessary.

✺ TO ASSEMBLE: Thread an artichoke piece, followed by 1 cherry tomato half or whole, and a piece of mozzarella onto each skewer. Repeat the process until all the ingredients have been used. Transfer to a platter and serve.

DO-AHEAD TIPS: Assemble the skewers, cover with plastic wrap, and refrigerate up to 1 day in advance. Serve as directed.

This skewer screams Martini soiree. Smoked salmon is a timeless hors d'oeuvre unmatched when paired with flirtatious little cocktail onions and then bathed in our feisty cream cheese mixture. When serving these devilish rolls, consider decorating the plate with caperberries and delicate twists of lemon zest.

CREAM CHEESE MIXTURE:

5 ounces cream cheese at room
    temperature

⅓ cup bread and butter pickles,
    finely chopped

3 tablespoons finely chopped
    cocktail onions

1 tablespoon prepared horseradish

1 tablespoon chopped fresh dill

Four 6-inch flour tortillas
    (preferably spinach-, tomato-,
    or herb-flavored)

3 ounces smoked salmon, coarsely
    chopped

24 fresh dill sprigs for garnish

MAKES ABOUT 25 ROULADES

Smoked Salmon, Cream Cheese, and Martini Onion Roulades

✹ TO MAKE THE CREAM CHEESE MIXTURE: Stir together the cream cheese, pickles, onions, horseradish, and dill in a small bowl. Refrigerate for at least 15 minutes so the flavors marry.

✹ TO ASSEMBLE: Divide the cream cheese mixture evenly among the tortillas (about 3 tablespoons each) and spread, leaving a 1-inch border. Sprinkle one fourth of the salmon evenly on top of the cream cheese mixture on each tortilla. Roll each tortilla into a tight roll and place, seam-side down, on a cutting board. Using a serrated knife, cut off the ends of each roll and slice into ¾-inch-thick pieces. Secure each piece with a toothpick. Place on serving plate, filling-side up, and garnish with a dill sprig.

DO-AHEAD TIPS: The cheese mixture can be made up to 3 days in advance. The tortillas can be rolled 1 day in advance, wrapped in plastic wrap, refrigerated, and cut 6 to 8 hours before serving. Skewer and serve slightly chilled.

Salami, Pepperoncini, and Jack Cheese with Lemon-Oregano Essence

This is an antipasto you can get around! Gone is the mound of meats and cheeses, replaced by a manageable sword of salami and cheese punctuated by tangy pepperoncini peppers. The lemon-oregano essence dresses up this humble appetizer, turning it into a sophisticated evening opener. Asiago, Parmesan, and mozzarella di bufula are excellent alternatives to Monterey Jack.

LEMON-OREGANO ESSENCE:

1 teaspoon fresh lemon juice

¼ teaspoon dried oregano

Pinch of kosher salt

Pinch of freshly ground pepper

1 tablespoon extra-virgin olive oil

2 ounces 2½-inch-diameter salami slices, each halved crosswise

Twenty-four ¾-inch pieces pepperoncini, seeded (6 to 12 peppers)

Twenty-four ½-by-1-by-¼-inch slices Jack cheese (about 4 ounces)

MAKES 24 SKEWERS

✳ TO MAKE THE ESSENCE: Combine the lemon juice, oregano, kosher salt, and pepper in a very small bowl. Using a fork, stir in the olive oil (or shake the ingredients together in a small jar). Set aside.

✳ TO ASSEMBLE: Place several halves of salami on a work surface, the straight edge closer to you. Place a piece of pepperoncini in the center of each salami slice. Top, vertically, with a piece of Jack cheese. Fold the left and right sides of the salami toward the center of the cheese and skewer with a decorative toothpick, creating a cone shape. Repeat the process until all ingredients have been used. Place the skewers on a plate and brush with the lemon-oregano essence. Transfer to a platter just before serving.

DO-AHEAD TIPS: The lemon-oregano essence can be prepared 1 day in advance and refrigerated. (Let sit at room temperature for at least 15 minutes before using.) The skewers can be assembled and refrigerated up to 1 day in advance. Brush with lemon essence and serve at room temperature.

Kabobs Revisited: *Big, Bold, and Delicious*

The recipes in this chapter are designed for those times when cocktail food just isn't enough. Pamper your boss, your in-laws, or special out-of-town guests with our sublime selection of skewered dinners. An opulent marriage of shrimp and scallops ingenuously threaded on fragrant stalks of lemongrass will captivate guests at any gathering. Meat-and-potato types won't be able to resist our robust steak pinwheel stuffed with red bell peppers nestled in pesto. Our spiced pork spear stacked with roasted garlic, bay leaf, and toothsome bits of marinated plum will woo finer palates. And romantic tête-à-têtes will finish in your favor when you ply the object of your desire with our lusty lamb, fig, and lemon confit kabob swirled in a scintillating mint dipping sauce. With this playful collection of veritable meals on a stick, sit-down dinners don't have to be stodgy.

Chicken Fondue with Sun-Dried Tomato Aioli and Curry Sauce

Fondue reminds us of sweater weather. This comforting and wonderfully intimate dish is perfect for a small gathering of close friends. Though fondue bourguignon, the traditional fried-meat fondue, calls for beef, we've created a variation using chicken instead. Don't hesitate to use leg of lamb, beef, or pork tenderloin. Skinless duck or turkey breast can easily be substituted for the chicken. Or, feel free to serve a selection of meats. We like to serve fondue with green salad, some crusty French bread, and a Zinfandel. Who says chicken has to be served with white wine?

YELLOW CURRY SAUCE:

1 teaspoon curry powder
½ teaspoon cumin powder
⅛ teaspoon ground turmeric
1 cup plain yogurt
2 tablespoons mango chutney
1 tablespoon chopped shallot
1 tablespoon chopped fresh cilantro
¼ teaspoon kosher salt

SUN-DRIED TOMATO AIOLI:

¾ cup commercial marinara sauce
⅓ cup mayonnaise
¼ cup oil-packed sun-dried tomatoes, drained and finely chopped
1 teaspoon balsamic vinegar
½ teaspoon chopped garlic
¼ teaspoon minced canned chipotle chile in adobo sauce

Vegetable shortening for deep-frying
4 skinless, boneless chicken breasts, cut into ¾-inch pieces, at room temperature (see note)

MAKES 4 SERVINGS

✽ TO MAKE THE CURRY SAUCE: Put the curry, cumin, and turmeric in a small sauté pan or skillet and toast over medium-high heat for about 30 seconds, or until the spices become fragrant. Be careful not to burn, or the spices will become bitter. Set aside. Combine the yogurt, chutney, shallot, cilantro, kosher salt, and toasted spices in a small bowl. Add more kosher salt, if necessary. Refrigerate for at least 1 hour for flavors to marry.

✽ TO MAKE THE AIOLI: Mix the marinara, mayonnaise, tomatoes, vinegar, garlic, and chile together in a bowl. Refrigerate for at least 1 hour for flavors to marry.

✽ Melt just enough vegetable shortening to fill a metal fondue pot about halfway. Heat on the kitchen stove over high heat until the oil reaches 375°F on a deep-frying thermometer. Transfer the fondue pot to a fondue burner with a high flame. Present the uncooked chicken pieces on a platter along with 4 metal fondue forks or wooden skewers. The chicken should be cooked until opaque in the center and slightly brown on the outside. Serve with the room-temperature sauces.

DO-AHEAD TIPS: The chicken can be sliced up to 1 day in advance and refrigerated. The sauces can be made 3 days in advance and brought to room temperature before serving.

NOTE: *Let the chicken sit at room temperature for at least 15 minutes before cooking to prevent it from splattering in the oil.*

Caesar Salad with Lemongrass-Skewered Shrimp and Scallops

Our recipe calls for a conservative amount of garlic, so if you're a lover of this powerful bulb, step up the quantity. Remember, however, that the older the garlic the stronger its flavor, so taste before you dose. Lemongrass is widely available at Asian markets, but if you can't find lemongrass, skewer the shrimp and scallops with wooden or metal skewers. Leftover dressing can be stored in the refrigerator for up to 1 week and used to dress up just about anything, from steamed vegetables to pasta salads.

✳ TO MAKE THE CAESAR DRESSING: Combine the mayonnaise, Parmesan, lemon juice, mustard, Worcestershire sauce, garlic, anchovy, and pepper in a small bowl. Whisk until well incorporated. Whisk in the water to desired consistency. Refrigerate until chilled.

✳ Preheat a grill to medium high or the oven to 450°F. Toss the shrimp with 2 teaspoons of the olive oil in a small bowl. In a separate bowl, gently toss the scallops with the remaining 2 teaspoons oil. Season the shrimp and scallops, on both sides, with kosher salt and pepper. Thread 4 shrimp onto each of 4 lemongrass skewers, threading them through the head and tail so they will lie flat when cooking. Thread 4 scallops onto each of the remaining 4 lemongrass skewers, so they will also lie flat when cooking. Cover the grill and cook for 8 minutes, rotating the skewers frequently, until the shrimp are pink and the scallops are opaque throughout. Or, place the skewers on

CONTINUED

CAESAR DRESSING:

1 cup mayonnaise

¼ cup Parmesan cheese, preferably Reggiano

1 tablespoon plus 1 teaspoon fresh lemon juice

1 tablespoon Dijon mustard

2 teaspoons Worcestershire sauce

2 teaspoons minced garlic

2 anchovy fillets, finely chopped (about 1 teaspoon)

⅛ teaspoon ground pepper

About ⅓ cup water for thinning

16 large shrimp (about 1 pound), peeled and deveined (tails on)

1 tablespoon plus 2 teaspoons olive oil

16 medium sea scallops (about 1 pound), muscles removed

¾ teaspoon kosher salt

¼ teaspoon ground pepper

8 stalks lemongrass, cut into 10- to 12-inch skewers, soaked in water for 30 minutes (see page 13)

2 cups croutons

6 cups lightly packed mixed salad greens

6 cups lightly packed chopped hearts of romaine

1 cup grated Parmesan cheese, preferably Reggiano

MAKES 8 SKEWERS;
SERVES 4 AS AN ENTRÉE

a baking sheet lined with aluminum foil and bake for 8 to 10 minutes on the top rack of the oven.

❀ TO ASSEMBLE: **Toss the croutons in a bowl with about ¼ cup of the dressing. Add the greens and lettuce and Parmesan cheese. Add about ½ cup dressing. Season with more kosher salt and pepper to taste, if necessary. Divide among 4 serving plates. Criss-cross 2 seafood skewers on top of each salad portion.**

DO-AHEAD TIPS: The dressing can be made up to 1 week in advance and refrigerated. The seafood can be grilled or baked up to 8 hours in advance and refrigerated. (If precooked, be sure to cook the seafood on the rare side so as not to overcook it when reheated.) Reheat in a preheated 350°F oven, covered with aluminum foil, for about 5 minutes.

Mahimahi, Pineapple, and Bell Pepper Brochettes with Cilantro Sauce

Magnify the tropical flavor of this dish by piling the kabobs on a bed of coconut-accented jasmine rice. Ordinary rice is made memorable with the simple addition of coconut milk and toasted shredded coconut. For extra decadence, sprinkle in a handful of ground macadamia nuts, then close your eyes and head for the islands. If mahimahi is not available, swordfish or shark make good stand-ins.

CILANTRO SAUCE:

1½ cups firmly packed fresh cilantro
   leaves
¾ cup unsweetened coconut milk
2 tablespoons firmly packed brown
   sugar
1 tablespoon fresh lime juice
1 tablespoon fish sauce
½ teaspoon green curry paste
   (see page 18)
½ teaspoon minced garlic

Twenty-four 1½-by-1½-by-½-inch
   pieces mahimahi (about
   1½ pounds)
3 tablespoons vegetable oil
Twenty-four 1½-by-½-inch wedges
   fresh pineapple
Twenty-four 1½-inch squares red bell
   pepper (2 medium)
1¼ teaspoons kosher salt
½ teaspoon ground pepper

MAKES 8 SKEWERS;
SERVES 4 AS AN ENTRÉE

✸ Select eight 10- to 12-inch metal or wooden skewers; soak wooden ones in water for 30 minutes and drain before use.

✸ TO MAKE THE SAUCE: Combine the cilantro, coconut milk, brown sugar, lime juice, fish sauce, green curry paste, and garlic in a blender. Blend until smooth. Set aside.

✸ Preheat a grill to medium high or the oven to 400°F. Place the mahimahi in a medium bowl. Toss with 1 tablespoon of the vegetable oil. Place the pineapple and red pepper in a separate bowl. Toss with the remaining 2 tablespoons oil. Thread a piece of pineapple, followed by a piece of fish and a piece of red bell pepper, on a skewer. Repeat the process 2 more times. Repeat with the remaining skewers. Season each skewer with kosher salt and pepper, rotating the kabobs to season evenly.

✸ Cover the grill and cook until the fish is opaque throughout, about 12 minutes, turning at least once. Or, place the skewers on a baking sheet lined with aluminum foil in the center of the oven for about 12 minutes. Serve the skewers immediately, with the sauce.

DO-AHEAD TIPS: The cilantro sauce can be made 2 days in advance and brought to room temperature before serving. The skewers can be assembled and refrigerated 1 day in advance. In this case, do not toss them with oil. Pat each skewer dry with a paper towel, brush all sides with oil, and season with kosher salt and pepper just before cooking.

Lamb, Figs, and Lemon Confit with Mint-Yogurt Dipping Sauce

We created this splendid skewer as our tribute to the Mediterranean. Its intense, sun-drenched flavor is best when buoyed by a bed of warm bulgur or couscous tossed liberally with olive oil, mint, and toasted pine nuts. If figs aren't at their prime, rehydrated dried figs also work well (see note).

LEMON CONFIT:
Twenty-four ½-inch-thick lemon
    wedges (about 2 large lemons)
1 cup olive oil

MINT-YOGURT DIPPING SAUCE:
1 cup plain yogurt
3 tablespoons chopped fresh mint
2 tablespoons minced red onion
½ teaspoon ground cumin
¼ teaspoon kosher salt

MARINADE:
2 tablespoons chopped fresh mint
2 teaspoons ground cumin
½ teaspoon ground cinnamon
½ teaspoon ground pepper
¼ teaspoon ground nutmeg
2 teaspoons minced garlic
¼ cup reserved lemon oil from
    lemon confit, above

Twenty-four 1½-inch pieces lean
    boned leg of lamb (about
    1½ pounds, trimmed)
12 fresh figs, halved lengthwise
1¼ teaspoons kosher salt

MAKES 8 SKEWERS;
SERVES 4 AS AN ENTRÉE

❊ Select eight 10- to 12-inch metal or wooden skewers; soak wooden ones in water for 30 minutes and drain before using.

❊ TO MAKE THE LEMON CONFIT: Spread the lemon wedges in a single layer in a large nonreactive saucepan and cover with the olive oil. Cook over low heat (never bringing to a boil) until the lemons are somewhat soft and the oil is infused with lemon flavor, about 10 minutes. Set aside to cool. Strain, reserving the lemons and the flavored oil. Leftover oil may be used in salad dressings and drizzled over steamed vegetables, fish, meat, or pasta.

❊ TO MAKE THE MINT-YOGURT SAUCE: Mix the yogurt, mint, red onion, cumin, and kosher salt together in a small bowl. Refrigerate until ready to use.

❊ TO MARINATE THE LAMB: Combine the mint, cumin, cinnamon, pepper, nutmeg, garlic, and lemon oil in a medium bowl. Add the lamb and toss to coat until the spices are evenly distributed. Marinate for at least 15 minutes.

❊ Preheat a grill to medium high or the oven to 400°F.

❊ TO ASSEMBLE: Thread a lemon wedge (through the rind), followed by a piece of lamb and a fig half on a skewer. Repeat the process 2 more times. Repeat with the remaining skewers. Season with the salt, rotating to season evenly. Place the skewers on a grill rack. Cover grill and cook for 10 to 12 minutes, rotating frequently, until the lamb is pink in

CONTINUED

the center. Or, place the skewers on a baking sheet lined with aluminum foil and bake for about 10 minutes in the center of the oven. Serve the skewers with the dipping sauce.

DO-AHEAD TIPS: The lemon confit can be made 2 days in advance. The mint-yogurt sauce can be made 1 day in advance. The skewers can be assembled 1 day in advance. Let the meat come to room temperature and cook as directed.

NOTE: *To rehydrate dried figs, place the figs in a small bowl and cover with boiling water. Cover with plastic wrap and let sit until soft, about 10 minutes. Drain the figs and halve lengthwise.*

London Broil, Yellow Bell Pepper, Shiitake, and Red Onion Kabobs

We love shiitakes in this recipe, but white mushrooms cut in half make a great, economical alternative. Tender cubes of chicken, pork, and lamb also work well in this recipe, especially when heaped atop a generous mound of mashed potatoes garnished with a sprig of fresh rosemary. If you choose to substitute chicken, prepare the marinade with white wine instead of red. To save time, purchase a bottle of your favorite herbed vinaigrette to replace our marinade.

HERBED MARINADE:

1 cup olive oil

½ cup chopped red onion

¼ cup red wine

¼ cup balsamic vinegar

2 tablespoons fresh rosemary leaves

2 cloves garlic, smashed

Twenty-four 1½-inch pieces London
broil (about 1½ pounds,
trimmed)

Twenty-four 1½-inch pieces red
onion (one layer, not a "stack")

Twenty-four 1½-inch pieces yellow
bell pepper

24 medium shiitake mushrooms,
stemmed

1 teaspoon kosher salt

¼ teaspoon ground pepper

MAKES 8 SKEWERS;
SERVES 4 AS AN ENTRÉE

❋ Choose eight 10-inch or 12-inch metal or wooden skewers; if using wooden ones, soak them in water for 30 minutes, then drain.

❋ TO MAKE THE MARINADE: Combine the olive oil, red onion, red wine, balsamic vinegar, rosemary, and garlic in a blender and blend until smooth. Set aside.

❋ TO ASSEMBLE: Thread a piece of London broil, followed by a piece of red onion, yellow pepper, and shiitake on a skewer. Repeat the process 2 more times. Place the skewers in a glass baking dish or a self-sealing plastic bag and add the marinade. Make sure the kabobs are evenly coated. Marinate for at least 15 minutes at room temperature, or up to 8 hours in the refrigerator.

❋ Preheat a grill to medium high or an oven to 400°F. Place the kabobs on a paper towel–lined plate and pat dry, using a paper towel. Season with kosher salt and pepper, rotating the kabobs to season evenly. Place the skewers on a grill rack that has been brushed or sprayed with oil.

❋ Cover the grill and cook for 5 to 6 minutes on each side for medium rare, or until the meat is the desired doneness. Or, place on a baking sheet lined with aluminum foil and bake in the center of the oven for about 13 minutes. Serve immediately.

DO-AHEAD TIPS: The skewers can be assembled and marinated 6 to 8 hours in advance. Cook just before serving.

Pinwheel Steaks with Basil-Parsley Pesto and Roasted Red Peppers

Like most steaks, this substantial pinwheel tastes best when coupled with a dense, buttery baked potato. Add a ragout of wild mushrooms and pour a glass of well-aged Cabernet for an opulent seated dinner.

PESTO:

1½ cups firmly packed fresh basil
    leaves

1 cup firmly packed fresh parsley
    leaves

2 teaspoons chopped garlic

3 tablespoons olive oil

¾ cup grated Parmesan cheese,
    preferably Reggiano

⅓ cup pine nuts, toasted

⅛ teaspoon ground pepper

Kosher salt to taste

PESTO DRIZZLE:

⅓ cup pesto (above)

¼ cup high-quality extra-virgin
    olive oil

3 tablespoons water

1 tablespoon fresh lemon juice

Kosher salt to taste

Two 12-ounce New York strip steaks
    (about 1 inch thick)

1 teaspoon kosher salt

½ teaspoon pepper

⅔ cup roasted red peppers (see
    page 21)

2 tablespoons vegetable oil

MAKES 4 PINWHEELS;
SERVES 4 AS AN ENTRÉE

❋ Select eight 10- to 12-inch metal or wooden skewers; soak wooden ones in water for 30 minutes and drain before use.

❋ TO MAKE THE PESTO: Combine the basil, parsley, garlic, and oil in a food processor and process to a coarse mixture. Shut the motor off and add the Parmesan cheese, pine nuts, and ground pepper. Pulse until smooth and well incorporated. Season with kosher salt.

❋ TO MAKE THE PESTO DRIZZLE: Whisk together ⅓ cup of the pesto with the olive oil in a small bowl. Whisk in the water and lemon juice. Season with salt. Set aside.

❋ Preheat the oven to 475°F. Line a baking sheet with aluminum foil.

❋ TO ASSEMBLE: Trim any excess fat from the meat and pat the meat dry. Sandwich the steaks between 2 pieces of plastic wrap. Place the steaks, vertically, on a work surface. Pound each steak, using a mallet or a heavy pan, until half as thick, about ½ inch. Remove the plastic wrap and season the steaks with ½ teaspoon of the kosher salt and ¼ teaspoon of the pepper. Spread each steak evenly with half the remaining pesto (about ⅓ cup per steak). Spread half the red peppers in a single layer over each pesto-covered steak. Roll the steaks up tightly. Slice each roll in half and skewer each of them crosswise with 2 skewers so the pinwheel will not unravel.

❋ Season the pinwheels evenly on all sides with the remaining ½ teaspoon kosher salt and remaining

CONTINUED

¼ teaspoon pepper. Brush the prepared pan with 1 tablespoon of the vegetable oil. Place the pinwheels on the pan and brush with the remaining 1 tablespoon oil. Bake in the center of the oven for about 15 minutes for medium rare, or until an instant-read thermometer registers 120°F when inserted in the center of pinwheel. Serve each pinwheel with a spoonful of the pesto drizzle alongside.

DO-AHEAD TIPS: The pesto can be made 1 week in advance and covered with a thin layer of oil. The drizzle and the pinwheels can be assembled 1 day in advance. If the pinwheels are being made a day in advance, don't season the meat with salt before rolling; simply season the meat on all sides just before cooking. Bring to room temperature and bake as directed.

Stunning on buffets and positively regal perched atop a bed of buttery couscous and sautéed spinach, this skewer possesses a wealth of exquisite flavor. If you aren't a plum-lover, substitute fresh ripe pineapple, dried apricots, or dried peaches, making sure to plump the dried fruits in boiling water, then toss them in oil to prevent burning. Frozen cranberry concentrate can be found in the frozen food section of most grocery stores. Although bay leaves aren't edible, they shouldn't be left out, as they give the pork wonderful flavor and add aesthetic appeal.

ROASTED GARLIC:

24 medium garlic cloves, peeled
(see note)
1 teaspoon olive oil

MARINADE:

½ cup frozen cranberry concentrate,
room temperature
½ cup honey
½ teaspoon ground cinnamon
¼ teaspoon ground pepper
¼ teaspoon ground allspice

6 ripe yet firm plums (red or black),
cut into quarters
Twenty-four 1½-inch cubes boneless
pork loin (about 1½ pounds,
trimmed)
24 fresh or dried bay leaves
1¼ teaspoons kosher salt

MAKES 8 SKEWERS;
SERVES 4 AS AN ENTRÉE

NOTE: *Peeling garlic cloves can be made easier by soaking them in water for 15 minutes to loosen their skins.*

✳ Choose eight 8- to 10-inch wooden or metal skewers; if using wooden ones, soak in water for 30 minutes and drain before using.

✳ TO MAKE THE ROASTED GARLIC: Preheat the oven to 350°F. Line a baking sheet with aluminum foil. Toss the garlic cloves and the olive oil in a small bowl. Spread evenly on the prepared pan and bake until golden brown and somewhat soft, about 20 minutes.

✳ TO MARINATE THE PORK AND PLUMS: Whisk together the cranberry concentrate, honey, cinnamon, pepper, and allspice in a medium bowl. Remove ⅓ cup of the marinade and toss with the plums in a small bowl. Toss the pork in the remaining marinade. Marinate for at least 15 minutes or up to 1 hour.

✳ TO ASSEMBLE: Preheat a grill to medium high or the oven to 400°F. Thread a roasted garlic clove, followed by a piece of pork, a bay leaf, and a piece of plum, on a skewer. Repeat the process 2 more times. Repeat with the remaining skewers. Season with the kosher salt. Cover the grill and cook for 10 to 12 minutes, rotating the skewers frequently, until the pork is just slightly pink in the center. Or, place skewers on a baking sheet lined with aluminum foil and bake in the center of the oven for about 10 minutes. Serve immediately.

DO-AHEAD TIPS: The roasted garlic can be made up to 2 days in advance. The marinade can be made 1 day in advance. The skewers can be assembled 4 to 6 hours before cooking.

Mushroom, Red Pepper, and Squash Yakitori

Japanese street vendors do a mean business in yakitori, *literally "grilled chicken." There, chicken parts are skewered and grilled over live coals and continuously basted with a slightly sweet soy-based sauce. In the California spirit, we've taken the liberty to vary this delicious dish, creating a simple combo of veggies that we grill and baste with our flashy ginger-infused glaze. Fried brown rice with green peas makes a great complement to the dish. Splash some of the yakitori glaze over the stir-fry to season it while it cooks.*

YAKITORI GLAZE:

⅔ cup low-salt vegetable stock

¼ cup sake

3 tablespoons soy sauce

3 tablespoons mirin or dry sherry

1 tablespoon packed brown sugar

2 teaspoons seasoned rice vinegar

2 small garlic cloves, thinly sliced

1 teaspoon minced fresh ginger

1 tablespoon cornstarch

1 tablespoon water

20 large white or cremini mush-
    rooms (about 2-inch caps)

Twenty 1¾-by-1-inch rectangular
    pieces yellow crookneck squash
    (about 3 medium squash)

Twenty-eight 1½-inch squares red
    bell pepper (about 3 large bell
    peppers)

⅓ cup vegetable oil for brushing

MAKES 12 SKEWERS;
SERVES 4 AS AN ENTRÉE

✽ Select twelve 10- to 12-inch wooden or metal skewers; if using wooden skewers, soak them in water for 30 minutes and drain before using.

✽ TO MAKE THE GLAZE: Combine the vegetable stock, sake, soy sauce, mirin, brown sugar, rice vinegar, garlic, and ginger in a medium nonreactive saucepan and bring to a boil over high heat. Dissolve the cornstarch in the water and whisk into the soy mixture. Boil for 1 minute. Remove from heat and set aside.

✽ Preheat a grill to medium high or the oven to 450°F.

✽ TO ASSEMBLE: Thread 5 mushrooms, lengthwise (starting with the bottom of each stem), onto each of 4 skewers. Thread 5 pieces of squash onto each of 4 other skewers and thread 7 red pepper pieces onto each of 4 other skewers. Place the kabobs on a baking sheet and brush with the vegetable oil, rotating the kabobs to coat evenly. Place the kabobs on the grill, grouping each type of vegetable for consistent cooking times. Close the grill and cook until the vegetables are tender, 10 to 20 minutes. (The vegetables have slightly different cooking times, so check them frequently for doneness.) Rotate the kabobs at least twice so the vegetables cook evenly. Brush liberally with the yakitori glaze a few minutes before the vegetables are ready. (Or, place the skewers on two baking sheets lined with aluminum foil and bake in the center of the oven for 25 to 35 minutes, basting at least twice after about 20 minutes.)

CONTINUED

❉ Remove from the grill or oven and brush vegetables liberally with the glaze. Serve immediately, drizzled with additional glaze.

DO-AHEAD TIPS: The yakitori glaze can be made 1 week in advance. The skewers can be assembled 1 day in advance and brushed with oil just before cooking. They can also be cooked as directed 1 day in advance and reheated just before serving.

Sweet-Tooth Satisfiers

Sweet tooths rejoice! This chapter showcases a multitude of skewered grand finales worthy of standing ovations. Meals and cocktail parties will end with a splash when dessert makes its entrance on a stick. From our vibrant Cantaloupe and Blackberry Skewers with Raspberry-Crème Swirl to our home-style Coconut Tapioca Custard with Tropical Fruits and Apricot Syrup, we've come up with something for everyone. Those in the fruit camp will be wowed by our great green skewer of Honeydew, Mint, and Kiwis with Lime-Yogurt Dipping Sauce, while those with a chocolate habit will get their fix from our Fudge Brownies with Miniature Candy Canes, or our cocoa-dusted Mini Ice-Cream Sandwiches with Raspberies. There are even Chocolate-Covered Banana Sicles with Peanut Sprinkles, to satisfy your inner child. Served as the perfect conclusion to a skewered meal or presented as the whimsical close to a more conventional menu, these hand-held desserts are sure to be applauded. Everyone's a sucker for a sweet ending.

Honeydew, Mint, and Kiwis with Lime-Yogurt Dipping Sauce

Ladies who lunch love light, sweet endings, so win them over with a dessert that won't do them in! This cool, elegant fruit skewer showcases summer's flavors, combining smooth melon with assertive mint and lively kiwi—but almost any fruit combination will do. Experiment with the season's freshest fruits, and vary the yogurt flavors too.

YOGURT DIPPING SAUCE:

1 cup vanilla yogurt

1 tablespoon frozen orange juice
　　concentrate

¾ teaspoon minced lime zest

24 kiwi triangles (about 2 kiwis)
　　(see note)

24 small fresh mint leaves

Twenty-four ½-inch honeydew balls

MAKES 24 SKEWERS

※ Choose twenty-four 6-inch wooden or decorative skewers; if using wooden ones, soak them in water for 30 minutes and drain before using.

※ TO MAKE THE SAUCE: Combine the yogurt, orange juice concentrate, and lime zest in a small bowl. Mix well. Refrigerate for at least 30 minutes so the flavors will marry.

※ TO ASSEMBLE: Slide a piece of kiwi onto each skewer, followed by a mint leaf and a honeydew ball. Refrigerate until chilled. Serve with the yogurt dipping sauce.

DO-AHEAD TIPS: The dipping sauce can be prepared 3 days in advance. The fruit can be prepared, but not assembled, up to 1 day in advance. The skewers can be assembled up to 4 hours in advance.

NOTE: *Using a sharp paring knife, cut a thin slice off both ends of each kiwi to reveal the flesh, then peel by cutting vertical strips from one end to the other. Cut each kiwi in half lengthwise, then cut each half in half again lengthwise. Cut each quarter crosswise into three ½-inch-thick pieces.*

Mini Ice-Cream Sandwiches with Raspberries

We prefer unsweetened cocoa powder in this recipe, but if you're a milk-chocolate lover or are preparing this for a young audience, sweetened cocoa powder may prove a safer bet. We've sold dozens of these desserts made with the classic vanilla ice-cream sandwich. But every now and then, Neapolitan ice-cream sandwiches offer an irresistible change of pace.

Cocoa powder for dusting
4 ice-cream sandwiches (5 by
    2 inches)
24 fresh raspberries

MAKES 24 SKEWERS

✳ TO ASSEMBLE: Sprinkle the cocoa powder liberally on a cutting board lined with waxed paper. Place an ice-cream sandwich directly on the cocoa powder–dusted waxed paper. Using a very sharp knife, cut each ice-cream sandwich in half lengthwise, then crosswise into ten 1-inch pieces. Spear a piece of ice-cream sandwich (cookie-side first) onto each skewer. Place the skewers on a baking sheet lined with waxed or parchment paper and freeze until just ready to serve. Thread 1 raspberry onto each skewer, and transfer the skewers to a serving platter. Serve immediately.

DO-AHEAD TIPS: The skewers can be assembled, covered with plastic wrap, and frozen 1 day in advance. Garnish with raspberries, as directed, just before serving.

A fitting grand finale on any cocktail buffet, strawberry shortcake ranks way up there on everyone's list of favorites. In this recipe, the cake gets updated with our lemony sour cream dipping sauce. Let Sara Lee come to your rescue if you're in a hurry, or purchase bakery lady fingers instead. Store-bought sweets are easily made over with the addition of fresh-picked berries and our delicately sweetened sour cream.

LEMONY SOUR CREAM:

1 cup sour cream

¼ cup sugar

1 teaspoon grated lemon zest

Pinch of kosher salt

LEMON POPPY SEED POUND
    CAKE:

2 cups sifted cake flour (sift
    before measuring)

2 tablespoons poppy seeds

1 teaspoon grated lemon zest

¾ teaspoon kosher salt

¾ teaspoon baking powder

5 large eggs

1½ teaspoons vanilla

1 cup (2 sticks) butter,
    at room temperature

1¼ cups sugar

16 small fresh strawberries, halved
    lengthwise

3 tablespoons strawberry jam

MAKES 32 SKEWERS

✺ TO MAKE THE LEMONY SOUR CREAM: Whisk together the sour cream, sugar, lemon zest, and kosher salt in a small bowl. Refrigerate so the flavors will marry.

✺ TO MAKE THE POUND CAKE: Preheat the oven to 325°F. Butter and lightly flour a 9-by-5-inch loaf pan. Stir together the flour, poppy seeds, zest, kosher salt, and baking powder in a small bowl. Set aside. Whisk together the eggs and the vanilla in a small bowl and set aside. Cream the butter in a mixer fitted with a paddle attachment for about 1½ minutes on medium speed, or until light and fluffy. Gradually beat in the sugar. Scrape down the sides of the bowl and beat 1 minute more. Add one third of the egg mixture and stir in until barely incorporated. Add one third of the flour mixture and stir until barely incorporated. Repeat the process, alternating the egg and flour mixture, until all the ingredients have been incorporated.

✺ Spoon the batter into the prepared pan and bake for 45 minutes to 1 hour, or until a toothpick inserted into the center comes out with tiny crumbs attached. Do not overcook or cake will be dry. Let cool in the pan on a rack for about 10 minutes. Slide a knife around the edges of the pan to make sure the cake doesn't stick. Invert the cake onto a cake rack. Reinvert so the cake is right-side up and let cool completely.

✺ Cut the cake in half vertically and reserve one of the halves for other uses (only half of the cake will be needed for assembly). Trim the brown crusty sides away. Cut the cake half into four ¾-inch-thick slices. Cut each slice in half lengthwise and make 3 horizontal cuts in each to create eight ¾-inch cubes per slice. Repeat until 32 cubes of cake have been cut.

❋ TO ASSEMBLE: Gently toss the strawberries and jam together in a separate bowl. Using a spoon, transfer 1 strawberry half onto each cube of pound cake and drizzle any extra syrup on the cake. Spear the straw-berry-topped cake with a toothpick. Repeat this process to make 32 skewers. Refrigerate for at least 15 minutes. Serve with the lemony sour cream as a dipping sauce.

DO-AHEAD TIPS: The lemony sour cream can be prepared and refrigerated 3 days in advance, as it gets better over time. The cake can also be prepared up to 3 days in advance. The skewers can be assembled and refrigerated 4 to 6 hours in advance. Drizzle with a little extra jam to freshen their appearance.

This fantastic home-style dessert deserves a standing ovation when paired with these tropical fruit skewers. Woefully under-rated, tapioca custard turns majestic when complemented by delicately sweet papaya, and a golden syrup of apricots and rum. Serve this creamy dessert in cups or coconut shell bowls, or go infor-mal and pass it in a deep serving dish, garnished with the fruit skewers. Present the rum-spiked apricot jam in a creamer. If you can't find sugarcane for the skew-ers, use sixteen 6-inch wooden skewers, soaked in water for 30 minutes and drained.

TAPIOCA CUSTARD:

Two 14-ounce cans unsweetened
    coconut milk
2¼ cups whole milk
1 cup sugar
⅔ cup quick-cooking tapioca
1 teaspoon kosher salt
2 eggs
1 teaspoon vanilla extract
2 tablespoons light rum
⅛ teaspoon coconut extract

APRICOT SYRUP:

¾ cup apricot jam
2 tablespoons light or dark rum
1 tablespoon water
Pinch of kosher salt

Sixteen 1-inch pieces pineapple
Sixteen 1-inch pieces papaya, prefer-
    ably the salmon-pink-fleshed
    Solo Sunrise variety
Sixteen 1-inch pieces mango
Sixteen 6-inch sugarcane skewers
    (see page 13)

MAKES 8 SERVINGS

Coconut Tapioca Custard with Tropical Fruits and Apricot Syrup

✳ TO MAKE THE TAPIOCA CUS-TARD: Combine the coconut milk, milk, sugar, tapioca, and kosher salt in a medium saucepan. Let sit for 5 minutes. Meanwhile, lightly beat eggs in a small bowl and set aside. Place the tapioca mixture over high heat and bring to a rolling boil, whisking frequently in the beginning and con-stantly towards the end. Remove from heat. Gradually whisk 1 cup of the hot tapioca into the beaten eggs. Return the custard mixture to the saucepan. Cover and let sit for 5 minutes. The custard will thicken as it cools. Add the vanilla, rum, and coconut extract. Transfer the custard to 8 individual serving cups. Let cool for at least 15 minutes. Cover with plastic wrap and refrigerate until chilled.

✳ TO MAKE THE APRICOT SYRUP: Combine the apricot jam, rum, water, and kosher salt in a small bowl. Set aside.

✳ Preheat the oven to 475°F.

✳ TO ASSEMBLE: Thread 1 piece each of pineapple, papaya, and mango onto each skewer. Place in a 9-by-14-inch baking dish. Spoon the apricot syrup over the fruit. Bake for 10 minutes, or until the apricot mix-ture is bubbling. Place 2 warm fruit skewers crosswise atop each individ-ual portion of chilled tapioca and drizzle with remaining apricot syrup. Serve immediately.

DO-AHEAD TIPS: The custard can be made up to 3 days in advance. The fruit skewers can be assembled (without the jam) 1 day in advance, covered with plastic wrap, and refrigerated. Heat the glaze, spoon over the fruit, and cook as directed.

Chocolate-Covered Banana Sicles with Peanut Sprinkles

For the Fourth of July, we like to cut red, white, and blue striped straws in half and use them as skewers. These refreshing pick-me-ups can be assembled several days in advance and are perfect for dessert grazing. Kids love them as much as adults, so be sure to make more than you think you will need.

½ cup heavy cream
1 cup semisweet chocolate morsels
  (about 6 ounces)
1 cup finely chopped peanuts
2 ripe but firm bananas

MAKES 24 SKEWERS

VARIATION: *A variety of nuts will work well with this dish, most notably macadamia nuts and toasted walnuts. Another topping that is quite delicious is toasted coconut. Try adding a few drops of almond extract to the chocolate if using coconut as a sprinkle.*

❊ Cut 12 decorative straws in half, or choose 24 toothpicks. Bring the cream to a boil in a heavy nonreactive saucepan. Remove from heat. Add the chocolate morsels and whisk until the chocolate is melted.

❊ TO ASSEMBLE: Line a plate with waxed or parchment paper. Pour the nuts onto a plate. Slice the bananas into ½-inch rounds just before assembling. Transfer the banana rounds, several at a time, to the bowl of chocolate and stir with a fork until coated. Using a fork, transfer the dipped banana pieces, one at a time, to the plate of chopped nuts and cover both sides with nuts. (For best results, tap the fork, with the banana slice on it, against the side of the pan to release excess chocolate. Then drag the fork against the bowl to prevent chocolate dribbling onto the nuts.) Using a straw half or a toothpick, skewer each banana slice from the round side, like a lollypop (not through the peanut-coated side). Transfer to the paper-lined plate. Repeat the process until all the banana rounds are coated. Freeze until slightly frozen, about 30 minutes, and serve.

DO-AHEAD TIPS: These can be assembled and frozen up to 1 week in advance. Cover tightly with plastic wrap. Let thaw slightly before serving.

Cantaloupe and Blackberry Skewers with Raspberry-Crème Swirl

Brunches, showers, and cocktail parties will end on a high note when this colorful skewer arrives as dessert. Everyone loves fruit, and this make-ahead combination doesn't scrimp on sweetness. Use your imagination—honeydew melon, blackberries, watermelon, and kiwi fruit all make excellent variations on the theme.

RASPBERRY SAUCE:

2 cups fresh raspberries, or
    12 ounces unsweetened frozen
    raspberries, thawed
¼ cup sugar
2 tablespoons crème fraîche
1 teaspoon fresh lemon juice

Twenty-four fresh blackberries,
    chilled (about 1 cup)
Twenty-four ½-inch cantaloupe
    balls, chilled (1 cantaloupe)
1 tablespoon crème fraîche for
    garnish

MAKES 24 SKEWERS

❋ TO MAKE THE RASPBERRY SAUCE: Combine the raspberries, sugar, crème fraîche, and lemon juice in a blender. Blend until smooth. Strain through a sieve into a small bowl, pressing firmly on the mixture with a rubber spatula. Season with more sugar or lemon juice, if necessary. Refrigerate until chilled.

❋ TO ASSEMBLE: Slide a blackberry, followed by a piece of cantaloupe, onto each skewer. Refrigerate until chilled. Serve with the raspberry dipping sauce. To create a swirled effect, slightly aerate the crème fraîche by stirring it vigorously with a fork. Place the "lightened" crème fraîche in the center of the raspberry sauce. Insert a skewer in the center of the crème fraîche and draw it outward and inward in a continuous sweeping motion without lifting the skewer from the liquid, thus creating a swirl effect. (If this dish is being used for a passed dessert item, the swirled design can be freshened by stirring the sauce until the existing cream is incorporated. Start again with a new dollop of crème fraîche.)

DO-AHEAD TIPS: The raspberry sauce can be prepared 3 days in advance. Garnish with a crème fraîche swirl just before serving. The skewers can be assembled 1 day in advance if the blackberries are very fresh.

Fudge Brownies with Miniature Candy Canes

There's nothing like a wallop of chocolate so rich and fudgey it melts in your mouth. Add to it a festive breath-saver that doubles as a fanciful finishing touch, and you've got it made. With no sticky chocolate residue on your fingertips—and cool, refreshing breath for after-dinner kissing—this dessert was custom-made for dinner dates.

FUDGE BROWNIES:

1¼ cups semisweet chocolate chips
    (7 ounces)
¾ cup (1½ sticks) unsalted butter,
    cut into small pieces
1 cup sugar
3 large eggs
¼ teaspoon kosher salt
1½ teaspoons vanilla extract
⅔ cup all-purpose flour

Thirty-six 3-inch-long miniature
    candy canes
Confectioners' sugar for dusting

MAKES 36 BITE-SIZED BROWNIES

✳ TO MAKE THE BROWNIES: Preheat the oven to 350°F. Butter and flour an 8-inch square baking pan. In a double boiler, melt the chocolate and butter over medium-low heat until smooth. Remove from heat. Let cool to lukewarm.

✳ Combine the sugar, eggs, and kosher salt in a small, heavy saucepan. Whisk constantly over low heat until the sugar dissolves, about 2 minutes. Do not boil. Remove from heat. Whisk in the chocolate mixture and vanilla until barely incorporated. Whisk in the flour just until incorporated. Spread the batter in the prepared pan. Bake until a tester inserted into the center comes out with moist crumbs attached, about 25 minutes. Do not overcook. Transfer the pan to a wire rack and let cool completely.

✳ TO ASSEMBLE: Trim the edges of the brownies and remove the trimmings. Cut the brownies into thirty-six 1-inch squares. Transfer to a baking sheet and spear each brownie (from top to bottom) with the straight end of a candy cane. Present the brownies so that the candy canes are vertical. Place a heaping tablespoon of powdered sugar in a fine-meshed sieve and dust it over the skewered brownies.

DO-AHEAD TIPS: The brownies can be made 3 days in advance and stored in an airtight container. The candy canes can be inserted up to 24 hours in advance.

Fondue never fails to excite guests, yet too many hosts are reluctant to serve this easy-to-prepare dessert because they don't have a fondue pot or chafing dish. For informal get-togethers, simply present the warmed fondue in an ordinary dish; when it cools down, return it to the kitchen for a quick "nuke" in the microwave. If pineapple isn't your preference, vary your accompaniments using bite-sized bits of pound cake or pitted fresh cherries. Chocoholics must be forewarned: A milk-chocolate Toblerone version of this dish is addictive.

Twenty-four ¾-inch pieces pineapple
Twenty-four ¾-inch pieces kiwi
   (about 2 firm, ripe kiwis)
12 unhulled strawberries, for garnish

WHITE TOBLERONE FONDUE:
¾ cup heavy cream
Four 3½-ounce bars white Toblerone
   chocolate, finely chopped
3 tablespoons finely chopped
   macadamia nuts
1 tablespoon kirsch (see note)

MAKES 48 SKEWERS; SERVES 8

✳ TO ASSEMBLE: Spear the pineapple with 24 toothpicks and the kiwi pieces with another 24 toothpicks. Arrange the skewers on a platter, leaving space for the bowl of fondue. Garnish by interspersing the strawberries throughout the fruit medley for added color. Refrigerate until ready to serve.

✳ TO MAKE THE FONDUE: Bring the cream to a boil in a heavy non-reactive saucepan. Remove from heat and add the white chocolate. Let stand until the chocolate softens, about 5 minutes, and whisk together. The mixture will not be completely smooth, due to the nougat in the chocolate. Whisk in the nuts and the kirsch until incorporated. Transfer the warm chocolate to a microwave-safe glass bowl. Place in the center of the fruit platter. Serve immediately.

DO-AHEAD TIPS: The fondue can be made 3 to 5 days in advance and refrigerated. Just before serving, microwave it in 20-second increments until warm. Or, warm in a double boiler. Serve as directed.

NOTE: *Kirsch, a flavorful and traditional addition to fondue, is a clear brandy distilled from the juice and pits of cherries. Brandy makes a fine substitute.*

We've found the solution to avoiding mealtime stress with kids: Make it okay to eat with your hands! This collection of fun-filled finger foods, devised especially with the young ones in mind, is guaranteed to keep everyone happy. Youngsters will love our County Fair Corn Dogs and creamy Caramel Apples, and even Mom and Dad will devour our vitamin A—packed stack of sweet potatoes and fluffy marshmallows. Kids can get their feet wet in the kitchen when our gooey Peanut Butter, Rice Krispie, and Chocolate Chip Roll-ups are the order of the day. And a healthy dose of fruit is irresistible when it comes in the form of our icy Watermelon and Blueberry Popsicles. Whip up these recipes with their kid-friendly sticks, and watch in astonishment as the little ones in your life hound you for second helpings. (Keeping safety in mind, blunt the tips of skewers with kitchen shears. Or, use popsicle sticks or wooden dowels when appropriate.)

Corn dogs are best right out of the fryer, but who wants to deal with all that splatter while entertaining? We promise you your guests won't be disappointed if you fry before they arrive. In fact, these kid-friendly treats can even be precooked and frozen, making them the ideal party food—simply heat before serving. Vegetarians will devour tofu dogs, and turkey and chicken do justice to the recipe for those who prefer white meat. For a little extra kick, add a handful of chopped jalapeños to half the batter—the indulging adults at your party will thank you. If serving to children, blunt the tips of 8 wooden skewers using kitchen shears, or use wooden dowels or popsicle sticks.

CORNMEAL BATTER:
1 cup sifted all-purpose flour
    (sift before measuring)
½ cup yellow cornmeal
2 tablespoons sugar
1½ teaspoons baking powder
¾ teaspoon kosher salt
2 tablespoons vegetable shortening
    or cold butter, cut into
    pea-sized chunks
1 large egg, lightly beaten
½ cup plus 1 tablespoon milk

8 frankfurters
Vegetable oil for deep-frying
Ketchup, barbecue sauce, or
    mustard for serving

❋ Choose eight 12-inch dowels or wooden skewers: if using skewers, soak them in water for 30 minutes and drain. If serving to small children, blunt the tips of skewers with kitchen shears.

❋ TO MAKE THE CORNMEAL BATTER: Combine the flour, cornmeal, sugar, baking powder, and kosher salt in a medium bowl. Add the shortening or butter and mix with a fork until the mixture is crumbly. In a small bowl, whisk together the egg and milk. Add the egg mixture to the dry ingredients and mix until barely incorporated.

❋ TO ASSEMBLE: Coat a plate with oil. Pat the hot dogs dry and skewer each of them lengthwise (about three quarters of the way). Coat with batter as evenly as possible, using a spreading knife. (This step is similar to icing a cake.) Make sure to coat all parts of the hot dog, because any exposed areas will tend to burn. Place the battered hot dogs on the oiled plate.

❋ Add 2½ inches oil to a large saucepan. Heat the oil to 350°F. Add the batter-coated hot dogs in batches and cook until golden, about 3 minutes, rotating frequently. Transfer to paper towels to drain for about 5 minutes before serving. Serve hot, with condiments of choice.

DO-AHEAD TIPS: The cornmeal mixture can be made up to 8 hours in advance and refrigerated. The corn dogs can be assembled and frozen individually in oiled plastic wrap up to 2 weeks in advance (if frozen, let thaw 20 minutes before frying). The corn dogs can be fried up to 3 hours in advance and heated in a preheated 400°F oven, uncovered, for 6 to 8 minutes. Or, they can be fried, cooled completely, covered tightly with plastic wrap, and frozen up to 1 week in advance. Heat, unthawed, in a preheated 400°F oven for 10 minutes and serve immediately.

MAKES 8 CORN DOGS

You don't have to visit the fairground to enjoy a caramel apple—this recipe lets you and your kids make them at home with no guesswork and no candy thermometers. The apples in this recipe are skewered with cinnamon sticks, but there are plenty of alternatives, from popsicle sticks, dowels, and chopsticks to sturdy twigs and straws. (When skewering with straws, pierce the apples with 3 wooden skewers bound tightly together with tape, then cover the skewers with a red and white jumbo straw cut to size.) And, by all means, encourage the kids to get creative with decorating. Candy corn, M & M's, mini marshmallows, dried cranberries, raisins, and the like all work well. They can even personalize the apples with handmade name tags.

1 pound store-bought caramel candy
1 tablespoon water
1 tablespoon vanilla extract
⅛ teaspoon kosher salt
8 small red apples (about 4 ounces
    each), or 5 medium red apples
Eight 6-inch cinnamon sticks
    (see note)
¾ cup pecans, toasted and chopped

MAKES 8 CARAMEL APPLES

✸ Put the caramels, water, vanilla, and kosher salt in a double boiler over boiling water. Stir until caramels are melted and the mixture is smooth, about 10 minutes.

✸ Meanwhile, place 8 heavy (2-ply) cupcake liners on a baking sheet. Flatten them slightly so that the sides of the liners will not touch the sides of the apples. Spray the cupcake liners lightly with vegetable-oil cooking spray or brush with vegetable oil. Insert a cinnamon stick in the stem end of each apple. Place the chopped nuts in a shallow bowl.

✸ TO ASSEMBLE: Working quickly, tilt the bowl of warm caramel and dip 1 apple at a time into the mixture. Roll the apple so the caramel is evenly distributed over three quarters of the apple. Lift the apple from the caramel and let some of the caramel drip from the base. Scrape the excess caramel off on the side of the pan. Dip the base of each apple in the nuts and place on a cupcake liner. Decorate, if you like, before the caramel hardens; serve.

DO-AHEAD TIPS: If decorated, the apples should be eaten within a couple of hours. Otherwise, they can be made up to 1 day in advance, if humidity is not a factor.

NOTE: *Though many natural foods stores carry long cinnamon sticks, they may also be ordered from Penzey's Spices at 800-741-7787 or www.penzeys.com (4 ounces amounts to fifteen 6-inch sticks).*

Sweet Potato and Marshmallow Stix

The simple goodness of sweet potatoes punctuated by creamy marshmallows speaks for itself. This dish will be requested again and again—not just on Thanksgiving Day. It's an easily prepared alternative to sweet potato casserole, too often ruined by an overdose of nuts or alcohol.

2 medium sweet potatoes, peeled
    and cut into sixteen 2-inch
    cubes
1 tablespoon salted butter, melted
¼ teaspoon kosher salt
Pinch of ground cinnamon
    (optional)
Eight 6-inch-long cinnamon sticks
    (see note)
8 large marshmallows

MAKES 8;
SERVES 4 AS A SIDE DISH

❋ Preheat the oven to 400°F. Line a baking sheet with aluminum foil. Toss the sweet potato pieces in a small bowl with the butter. Season with the kosher salt and ground cinnamon, if desired. Toss until evenly coated and spread out on the prepared pan. Bake for about 20 minutes, or until tender when pierced with a skewer. (Do not overcook, or the sweet potatoes will become overly soft and may break when skewered.) Remove from the oven and let cool to the touch.

❋ Preheat the broiler. Line a baking sheet with aluminum foil.

❋ TO ASSEMBLE: Thread each cinnamon stick with 2 pieces of sweet potato and 1 marshmallow, starting and ending with the sweet potatoes. Place the skewers on the prepared pan and broil about 5 inches from the heat source for 45 seconds to 1 minute. (Warning: This cooking time is crucial, as the marshmallows can turn into a melted puddle if they are cooked any longer. Watch closely!) Serve immediately.

DO-AHEAD TIPS: These skewers can be assembled 1 day in advance and refrigerated. Bring the skewers to room temperature before cooking. Broil as directed.

NOTE: *Though many natural foods stores carry long cinnamon sticks, they may also be ordered from Penzey's Spices at 800-741-7787 or www.penzeys.com (4 ounces amounts to fifteen 6-inch sticks).*

Watermelon and Blueberry Popsicles

What would summer be without pop- sicles? Our fruity take on this all- American favorite offers all-natural goodness—no artificial dyes or fake fruit syrups. Popsicle molds can be found in drugstores and specialty cooking shops. The molds do vary in size, so if yours hold more than ¼ cup, double our recipe. White grape juice concentrate, available at most grocery stores in the frozen foods aisle, adds a significant amount of depth and body to these popsicles.

1¼ cups seeded diced watermelon
1½ cups fresh or thawed frozen
   blueberries
¼ cup sugar
3 tablespoons frozen white grape
   concentrate
1 tablespoon fresh lemon juice

MAKES 8 POPSICLES

❋ Combine the watermelon, 1 cup of the blueberries, sugar, white grape concentrate, and lemon juice in a blender. Puree until smooth. Fill each of 8 popsicle molds three-fourth full (about 3 tablespoons per mold). Add 1 tablespoon of the reserved blueberries to each mold, creating full molds. Place the lid/sticks on top. Freeze for 6 to 8 hours or overnight. Just before serving, run the molds under warm water for 10 to 15 sec- onds, and the popsicles will slide out of the molds with ease.

DO-AHEAD TIPS: The popsicles can be frozen up to 2 weeks in advance.

Peanut Butter, Rice Krispie, and Chocolate Chip Roll-ups

Rice Krispie treats have met their match with this gooey, crunchy roll-up. Adults and kids alike will pop pick after pick of these sinful spheres into their mouths without a second thought. Nutella, long a snack favorite in Europe, is a smooth chocolate hazelnut spread that blends magically with peanut butter, Rice Krispies, and chocolate. Purchase multi-grain tortillas for a wholesome variation, or send the chocolate quotient soaring by using chocolate tortillas.

½ cup crunchy peanut butter

Four 6-inch flour tortillas

¼ cup Nutella

⅓ cup Rice Krispies

⅓ cup chocolate morsels for
  garnish

MAKES ABOUT 24 ROLL-UPS

✸ TO ASSEMBLE: Spread 2 tablespoons peanut butter on each tortilla, leaving a 1-inch border. Spread 1 tablespoon of Nutella evenly on top of the peanut butter on each tortilla. Sprinkle each tortilla with 1 heaping tablespoon of Rice Krispies. Roll each tortilla into a tight roll and place, seam-side down, on a cutting board. Using a sharp knife, cut off the ends of each roll and slice into ¾-inch-thick pieces. Secure each piece with a toothpick. Place on a serving plate, filling-side up. Garnish each with 3 chocolate morsels.

DO-AHEAD TIPS: The tortillas can be rolled 1 day in advance, wrapped in plastic wrap, and left at room temperature. They can be cut, skewered, garnished, and covered with plastic wrap up to 2 hours before serving.

Cocktails and Swizzles

When you put out a cocktail spread worthy of special attention, go the extra mile to make sure your libations are up to par. In this chapter we offer our takes on some of America's favorite cocktails, and top them off with little garnish skewers that are long on style. In our opinion, drinks are at least half the equation when entertaining, so putting creative thought into their presentation is of prime importance. These snazzy swizzle skewers—kalamatas, cherry tomatoes, and celery for a Bloody Mary, raspberries and blueberries for a Cosmopolitan— provide a departure from the same old fruit wedge or olive garnish. They dress up drinks in a chic, simple way. Edible swizzles look great in the glass and on the bar. Beware! Once you serve them, there's no turning back. Your cocktails will seem naked without them.

Clamato is the secret ingredient in our version of this divine brunch favorite. A zesty tomato juice lightly infused with clam broth, Clamato makes an unbeatable Bloody. When it comes to skewered garnishes, the range for Bloody Marys is immense. Spike any type of olive, add a pickled onion, caperberry, or slice of lime, and you've got a great variation on our updated celery stick. For really racy Bloody Marys, freeze spiced tomato juice in an ice tray and plop the feisty cubes in the drink in place of ordinary ice.

GARNISH:

4 black olives, preferably kalamatas

4 cherry tomatoes, preferably
    Sweet 100's

4 celery stalks with leaves

2½ cups Bloody Mary mix,
    preferably Mr. and Mrs. T

1 cup Clamato juice

8 ounces vodka

2 tablespoons fresh lemon juice

1 tablespoon prepared horseradish

1 teaspoon Worcestershire sauce

½ teaspoon celery salt

Kosher salt and freshly ground
    pepper to taste

Ice cubes

SERVES 4

Bloody Marys

✳ TO ASSEMBLE THE GARNISH: Thread each of 4 toothpicks with 1 black olive and 1 tomato. Spike the top end of the celery stalk, creating an extension of the celery. The size of the tomatoes will vary; make sure the larger of the garnishes is on the bottom or else it will be top heavy.

✳ Whisk together all of the remaining ingredients except the ice cubes in a pitcher. Season with additional lemon juice, horseradish, kosher salt, and pepper to taste, if necessary. Fill four 12-ounce glasses with ice cubes and pour in the Bloody Mary mixture. Garnish with the skewers.

Topping off a blushing pink daiquiri with vivid slices of kiwi gives the drink a fanciful, tropical flair. Star fruit, also known as carombola, offers another innovative and colorful garnish. Or, combine both kiwi and star fruit with tender cubes of mango and a wee wedge of lime for a real showstopper.

Frozen Strawberry Daiquiris

GARNISH:

Two ¼-inch-thick kiwi slices, halved
    crosswise

2 unhulled fresh strawberries

1½ cups fresh strawberries, hulled
    and chopped

3 ounces light rum

¼ cup sugar

1 tablespoon fresh lime juice

¾ cup chopped frozen unsweetened
    strawberries

1½ cups crushed ice

SERVES 2

✺ TO ASSEMBLE THE GARNISH:
Thread each of two 6-inch wooden or decorative skewers with 1 piece of kiwi, followed by 1 strawberry and another kiwi piece.

✺ Place the chopped strawberries, rum, sugar, and lime juice in a blender. Blend until smooth. Add the frozen strawberries and ice. Blend until smooth. Pour into large margarita glasses or 12-ounce wine glasses and garnish with the skewers.

Feeling a bit Bacchanalian? Celebrate with a splash of tequila nobly garnished with a dangling cluster of frosty green grapes. The natural sugars of the grapes beautifully complement the sourness of a margarita. If you feel particularly festive (and ambitious), lightly brush the grapes with frothy egg whites and coat with sugar for a knock-out presentation.

4 clusters seedless green grapes
    (about 5 grapes per cluster)
1 lime wedge
Kosher salt for lining the rims
    of the glasses
4 ounces gold tequila
4 ounces Triple Sec
4 ounces fresh lime juice
¼ cup plus 1 tablespoon superfine
    sugar
Ice cubes

Margaritas

✻ Thread each of four 6-inch decorative skewers with a cluster of grapes, skewering at least 2 grapes within each cluster. Freeze if desired.

✻ Rub the rim of each of four margarita glasses with the lime wedge. Place the salt in a small saucer and dip the glasses into it. Pour the tequila, Triple Sec, lime juice, and sugar into a shaker filled with ice. Cover and shake well. Strain the margarita mixture into the prepared glasses and garnish with skewers.

SERVES 4

This sexy cocktail, so potent and pure, never goes out of style. Breathe new life into this timeless favorite by slightly tweaking its traditional green olive garnish. Replace the whole sphere with two cross-sections of a large stuffed olive speared side by side. The change in the garnish is minimal, but the results are stunning.

Martinis

2 large pimiento or sun-dried
    tomato–stuffed Spanish olives
    (about 1 inch in diameter)
4 ounces gin or vodka
Ice cubes
Whisper of vermouth

✻ Cut the olives in half crosswise and thread each of 2 decorative swizzles with 2 olive halves, side by side with the stuffing facing out.

✻ Fill a shaker with ice cubes and add the gin or vodka. Add the vermouth. Cover and shake. Drain the mixture into chilled martini glasses. Garnish with the skewers.

SERVES 2

A shocking red raspberry snuggled between two plump blueberries makes an unexpected addition to this popular cranberry cocktail. In the cooler months, when fresh cranberries are available, dip them in frothy egg white and coat with sugar for an equally elegant finish.

Cosmopolitans

GARNISH:
4 fresh blueberries
2 fresh raspberries

3 ounces vodka
2 ounces cranberry juice
1 ounce Triple Sec
1 teaspoon fresh lime juice
1 cup crushed ice

✳ TO ASSEMBLE THE GARNISH:
Thread each of two 6-inch wooden or decorative skewers with 1 blueberry, followed by 1 raspberry and another blueberry.
✳ Pour the vodka, cranberry juice, Triple Sec, and lime juice into a large shaker. Add the ice, cover, and shake. Pour into 2 chilled Martini glasses. Garnish with the skewers.

SERVES 2

This granddaddy of all bourbon drinks typically comes topped with a cherry. Create a new tradition by adding a wedge of fresh orange and a sprig of mint, then devour these bourbon-soaked skewers (in moderation)!

GARNISH:
2 fresh cherries
2 mint sprigs
One 1-inch-thick orange wedge,
    halved crosswise

4 ounces bourbon
1 ounce sweet vermouth
Dash of bitters (optional)
Ice cubes

Manhattans

✳ TO ASSEMBLE THE GARNISH:
Thread each of two 6-inch wooden or decorative skewers with 1 fresh cherry, followed by 1 mint sprig and 1 orange wedge.
✳ Combine the bourbon, sweet vermouth, optional bitters, and ice in a large mixing glass. Stir and strain into chilled cocktail glasses. Garnish with the skewers.

SERVES 2

Lime, mint, and pineapple team up as the bright companion skewer to our heady, rich piña colada cocktail. As pretty as it is perky on the palate, this contemporary garnish beats the tired maraschino cherry—topped orange slice hands down.

Piña Coladas

GARNISH:
Two ¼-inch-thick lime slices
2 large mint sprigs
Two ¾-inch-thick pineapple
     wedges with peel

8 ounces unsweetened pineapple
     juice
4 ounces light or dark rum
⅓ cup cream of coconut
2 cups crushed ice
1 tablespoon fresh lime juice

❋ TO ASSEMBLE THE GARNISH:
Thread each of two 6-inch wooden or decorative skewers with 1 lime slice, followed by 1 mint sprig and 1 pineapple wedge.
❋ Blend the pineapple juice, rum, cream of coconut, ice, and lime juice in a blender at high speed until frothy. Pour into two chilled 12-ounce cocktail glasses and garnish with the skewers.

SERVES 2

This cool smoothie version of traditional Spanish sangria is to die for. Ideal for poolside lounging and other warm-weather festivities, it makes a delectable "drinkable dessert" as well, and its geometric garnish will be gobbled up with unbridled enthusiasm.

GARNISH:
4 red grapes
1 orange slice, cut into quarters

¾ cup light fruity red wine,
     such as Beaujolais
⅓ cup lemon sorbet
1 cup red grapes, frozen
1 cup chopped fresh plums, frozen
1 tablespoon plus 1 teaspoon frozen
     orange concentrate

Sangria Smoothies

❋ TO ASSEMBLE THE GARNISH:
Thread 2 grapes and 2 orange quarters in alternating fashion on each of two 6-inch wooden or decorative skewers.
❋ Combine the red wine and lemon sorbet in a blender. Add the grapes, plums, and orange concentrate. Blend until smooth. Pour into two 12-ounce wineglasses and garnish with the skewers.

SERVES 2

Janet Torelli Handcrafted Silver
451 West Oakdale
Chicago, Illinois 60657
773-388-2388
www.martinipic.com
janet@martinipic.com

Niki Stix
www.nikistix.com
415-892-1150

Fillamento
2185 Fillmore St.
San Francisco, California 94115
415-931-2224

Handblock
42 Maine Street
Nantucket, Massachusetts 02554
508-228-4500
www.handblock.com

Hermes Vieau Design
539 Harvard
Houston, Texas 77007
713-861-5473

Crate & Barrel
125 Grant Avenue
San Francisco, California 94108
415-986-4000

A

Aioli
Lemony Tarragon Aioli, 40
Sun-Dried Tomato Aioli, 69
Apples, Caramel, 101
Apple Wood–Smoked Bacon-Wrapped
Scallops with Tamari Glaze, 30
Apricots
Apricot Syrup, 92
Smoked Duck with Spiced Apricots and
Watercress, 58
Artichokes
Cherry Tomatoes, Marinated Artichoke
Hearts, and Mozzarella, 64
Tuna with Black Olives and Marinated
Artichoke Crowns, 48
Asparagus
Asparagus Tips and New Potatoes, 54
Lobster and Asparagus with Lemony
Tarragon Aioli, 40
Avocado, Smoked Turkey, and Bacon with
Blue Cheese Vinaigrette, 43

B

Bacon
Apple Wood–Smoked Bacon-Wrapped
Scallops with Tamari Glaze, 30
Peppery Bacon-Wrapped Watermelon
Rind Pickles, 44
Smoked Turkey, Avocado, and Bacon with
Blue Cheese Vinaigrette, 43
Balsamic Sun-Dried Tomatoes, Broccoli, and
Smoked Gouda, 33
Banana Sicles, Chocolate-Covered, with
Peanut Sprinkles, 94
Basil-Parsley Pesto, 79
Beans
Green Beans and Carrot Disks, 54
Spicy Tofu with Cilantro and Smoky Black
Bean Dip, 47
Beef
Beef Satay, 42
London Broil, Yellow Bell Pepper, Shiitake,
and Red Onion Kabobs, 77
Pinwheel Steaks with Basil-Parsley Pesto
and Roasted Red Peppers, 79–80
Blackberry and Cantaloupe Skewers with
Raspberry Crème Swirl, 95
Bloody Marys, 107
Blueberry and Watermelon Popsicles, 104
Blue Cheese Vinaigrette, 43

B

Broccoli
Balsamic Sun-Dried Tomatoes, Broccoli,
and Smoked Gouda, 33
Broccoli Florets and Cherry Tomatoes, 54
Brownies, Fudge, with Miniature Candy
Canes, 97

C

Caesar Salad with Lemongrass-Skewered
Shrimp and Scallops, 70, 72
Cake, Lemon Poppy Seed Pound, 90
Candy canes
Fudge Brownies with Miniature Candy
Canes, 97
as skewers, 15
Cantaloupe
Cantaloupe and Blackberry Skewers with
Raspberry Crème Swirl, 95
Melon, Prosciutto, and Arugula with
Lime–Poppy Seed Vinaigrette, 61
Caramel Apples, 101
Caraway-Honey Mustard, 55
Carrot Disks and Green Beans, 54
Cheese
Balsamic Sun-Dried Tomatoes, Broccoli,
and Smoked Gouda, 33
Cherry Tomatoes, Marinated Artichoke
Hearts, and Mozzarella, 64
Curried Pimiento Cheese and Spinach
Pinwheels, 63
Eggplant, Chèvre, and Mint Rolls, 35
New Potatoes with Three-Cheese Fondue,
45
Open-Faced Mini Reubens, 52
Salami, Pepperoncini, and Jack Cheese
with Lemon-Oregano Essence, 67
Smoked Salmon, Cream Cheese, and
Martini Onion Roulades, 66
Smoked Turkey, Avocado, and Bacon with
Blue Cheese Vinaigrette, 43
Spanish Olive and Cream Cheese Spheres
on Red Pepper Squares, 62
Cherry Tomatoes, Marinated Artichoke
Hearts, and Mozzarella, 64
Chicken
Chicken Fondue with Sun-Dried Tomato
Aioli and Curry Sauce, 69
Chicken with Chutney and Macadamia
Nuts, 32
Cold Chicken, Mint, and Cucumbers with
Fiery Mango Dipping Sauce, 36

Chocolate
    Chocolate-Covered Banana Sicles with
        Peanut Sprinkles, 94
    Fudge Brownies with Miniature Candy
        Canes, 97
    Peanut Butter, Rice Krispie, and Chocolate
        Chip Roll-ups, 105
Cilantro Sauce, 73
Cinnamon sticks, 13, 15, 101, 102
Cocktails
    Bloody Marys, 107
    Cosmopolitans, 111
    Frozen Strawberry Daiquiris, 108
    Manhattans, 111
    Margaritas, 109
    Martinis, 109
    Piña Coladas, 112
    Sangria Smoothies, 112
Coconut
    Beef Satay, 42
    Coconut Tapioca Custard with Tropical
        Fruits and Apricot Syrup, 92
    Piña Coladas, 112
Cold Chicken, Mint, and Cucumbers with
    Fiery Mango Dipping Sauce, 36
Corn Dogs, County Fair, 100
Cosmopolitans, 111
County Fair Corn Dogs, 100
Crudité, 54
Cucumbers
    Cold Chicken, Mint, and Cucumbers with
        Fiery Mango Dipping Sauce, 36
    Radish Wheels and Cucumber Cubes, 54
Curried Pimiento Cheese and Spinach
    Pinwheels, 63
Custard, Coconut Tapioca, with Tropical
    Fruits and Apricot Syrup, 92

D
Daiquiris, Frozen Strawberry, 108
Dips
    Green Onion and Basil Dip, 53
    Smoky Black Bean Dip, 47
Drinking straws, 15
Duck, Smoked, with Spiced Apricots and
    Watercress, 58

E
Eggplant, Chèvre, and Mint Rolls, 35

F
Fiery Mango Dipping Sauce, 36
Figs, Lamb, and Lemon Confit with Mint-
    Yogurt Dipping Sauce, 74, 76
Fish
    Mahimahi, Pineapple, and Bell Pepper
        Brochettes with Cilantro Sauce, 73
    Moroccan-Spiced Swordfish with Red
        Peppers and Lemon Drizzle, 27
    Sesame-Crusted Salmon with Pineapple-
        Miso Sauce, 56
    Smoked Salmon, Cream Cheese, and
        Martini Onion Roulades, 66
    Tuna with Black Olives and Marinated
        Artichoke Crowns, 48
Fondue
    Chicken Fondue with Sun-Dried Tomato
        Aioli and Curry Sauce, 69
    White Toblerone Fondue with Kiwi and
        Pineapple Picks, 98
Frozen Strawberry Daiquiris, 108
Fudge Brownies with Miniature Candy
    Canes, 97

G
Garlic, roasting, 81
Glazed Shrimp with Bourbon Barbecue
    Dunk, 39
Glazed Strawberry Shortcakes with Lemony
    Sour Cream, 90–91
Green Beans and Carrot Disks, 54
Green Onion and Basil Dip, 53

H
Honeydew melon
    Honeydew, Mint, and Kiwis with Lime-
        Yogurt Dipping Sauce, 87
    Melon, Prosciutto, and Arugula with
        Lime–Poppy Seed Vinaigrette, 61

I
Ice-Cream Sandwiches, Mini, with
    Raspberries, 88

K
Kielbasa and Potatoes with Caraway-Honey
    Mustard, 55
Kiwis
    Honeydew, Mint, and Kiwis with Lime-
        Yogurt Dipping Sauce, 87

White Toblerone Fondue with Kiwi and Pineapple Picks, 98

L

Lacquered Pork with Water Chestnuts and Snow Peas, 51

Lamb
Lamb, Figs, and Lemon Confit with Mint-Yogurt Dipping Sauce, 74, 76
Lamb with Mint-Mustard Dipping Sauce, 34

Lemongrass, 13, 19

Lemons
Lamb, Figs, and Lemon Confit with Mint-Yogurt Dipping Sauce, 74, 76
Lemon Poppy Seed Pound Cake, 90
Lemony Sour Cream, 90–91
Lemony Tarragon Aioli, 40

Limes
Lime–Poppy Seed Vinaigrette, 61
Lime-Yogurt Dipping Sauce, 87

Lobster and Asparagus with Lemony Tarragon Aioli, 40

London Broil, Yellow Bell Pepper, Shiitake, and Red Onion Kabobs, 77

M

Macadamia Nuts, Chicken with Chutney and, 32

Mahimahi, Pineapple, and Bell Pepper Brochettes with Cilantro Sauce, 73

Mangoes
Coconut Tapioca Custard with Tropical Fruits and Apricot Syrup, 92
Fiery Mango Dipping Sauce, 36

Manhattans, 111

Margaritas, 109

Marshmallow and Sweet Potato Stix, 102

Martinis, 109

Melons. *See also* Watermelon
Cantaloupe and Blackberry Skewers with Raspberry Crème Swirl, 95
Honeydew, Mint, and Kiwis with Lime-Yogurt Dipping Sauce, 87
Melon, Prosciutto, and Arugula with Lime–Poppy Seed Vinaigrette, 61

Menus, 16

Mini Ice-Cream Sandwiches with Raspberries, 88

Mint-Mustard Dipping Sauce, 34

Mint-Yogurt Dipping Sauce, 74, 76

Moroccan-Spiced Swordfish with Red Peppers and Lemon Drizzle, 27

Mushrooms
London Broil, Yellow Bell Pepper, Shiitake, and Red Onion Kabobs, 77
Mushroom, Red Pepper, and Squash Yakitori, 82, 84
Mushrooms and Sweet Pearl Onions with Cabernet Syrup, 28

N

New Potatoes with Three-Cheese Fondue, 45

O

Olives
Spanish Olive and Cream Cheese Spheres on Red Pepper Squares, 62
Tuna with Black Olives and Marinated Artichoke Crowns, 48

Onions
London Broil, Yellow Bell Pepper, Shiitake, and Red Onion Kabobs, 77
Mushrooms and Sweet Pearl Onions with Cabernet Syrup, 28

Open-Faced Mini Reubens, 52

P

Papaya
Coconut Tapioca Custard with Tropical Fruits and Apricot Syrup, 92

Pasta
Spinach Tortellini with Roasted Red Pepper Pesto, 49

Pastrami
Open-Faced Mini Reubens, 52

Peanuts and peanut butter
Beef Satay, 42
Chocolate-Covered Banana Sicles with Peanut Sprinkles, 94
Peanut Butter, Rice Krispie, and Chocolate Chip Roll-ups, 105
Peanut Sauce, 42

Peppers
Curried Pimiento Cheese and Spinach Pinwheels, 63
London Broil, Yellow Bell Pepper, Shiitake, and Red Onion Kabobs, 77
Mahimahi, Pineapple, and Bell Pepper Brochettes with Cilantro Sauce, 73
Moroccan-Spiced Swordfish with Red Peppers and Lemon Drizzle, 27

Mushroom, Red Pepper, and Squash
Yakitori, 82, 84
Pinwheel Steaks with Basil-Parsley Pesto
and Roasted Red Peppers, 79–80
roasting, 21
Salami, Pepperoncini, and Jack Cheese
with Lemon-Oregano Essence, 67
Snow Pea Diamonds and Red Bell Pepper
Squares, 54
Spanish Olive and Cream Cheese Spheres
on Red Pepper Squares, 62
Spinach Tortellini with Roasted Red
Pepper Pesto, 49
Peppery Bacon-Wrapped Watermelon Rind
Pickles, 44
Pesto
Basil-Parsley Pesto, 79
Roasted Red Pepper Pesto, 49
Piña Coladas, 112
Pineapple
Coconut Tapioca Custard with Tropical
Fruits and Apricot Syrup, 92
Mahimahi, Pineapple, and Bell Pepper
Brochettes with Cilantro Sauce, 73
Piña Coladas, 112
Pineapple-Miso Sauce, 56
White Toblerone Fondue with Kiwi and
Pineapple Picks, 98
Pinwheel Steaks with Basil-Parsley Pesto and
Roasted Red Peppers, 79–80
Plums
Sangria Smoothies, 112
Spiced Pork with Plums, Roasted Garlic,
and Bay Leaves, 81
Popsicles, Watermelon and Blueberry, 104
Pork. See also Bacon; Prosciutto
Lacquered Pork with Water Chestnuts and
Snow Peas, 51
Spiced Pork with Plums, Roasted Garlic,
and Bay Leaves, 81
Potatoes
Asparagus Tips and New Potatoes, 54
Kielbasa and Potatoes with Caraway-
Honey Mustard, 55
New Potatoes with Three-Cheese Fondue,
45
Prosciutto, Melon, and Arugula with
Lime–Poppy Seed Vinaigrette, 61

R
Radish Wheels and Cucumber Cubes, 54
Raspberries
Cantaloupe and Blackberry Skewers with
Raspberry Crème Swirl, 95
Mini Ice-Cream Sandwiches with
Raspberries, 88
Reubens, Open-Faced Mini, 52
Roasted Red Pepper Pesto, 49
Roasted Yellow Squash and Zucchini with
Green Onion and Basil Dip, 53
Rosemary, 13

S
Salad, Caesar, with Lemongrass-Skewered
Shrimp and Scallops, 70, 72
Salami, Pepperoncini, and Jack Cheese with
Lemon-Oregano Essence, 67
Salmon
Sesame-Crusted Salmon with Pineapple-
Miso Sauce, 56
Smoked Salmon, Cream Cheese, and
Martini Onion Roulades, 66
Sangria Smoothies, 112
Satay, Beef, 42
Sauces. See also Pesto
Cilantro Sauce, 73
Fiery Mango Dipping Sauce, 36
Lime-Yogurt Dipping Sauce, 87
Mint-Mustard Dipping Sauce, 34
Mint-Yogurt Dipping Sauce, 74, 76
Peanut Sauce, 42
Pineapple-Miso Sauce, 56
Yellow Curry Sauce, 69
Sausage
Kielbasa and Potatoes with Caraway-
Honey Mustard, 55
Scallops
Apple Wood–Smoked Bacon-Wrapped
Scallops with Tamari Glaze, 30
Caesar Salad with Lemongrass-Skewered
Shrimp and Scallops, 70, 72
Sesame-Crusted Salmon with Pineapple-
Miso Sauce, 56
Shortcakes, Glazed Strawberry, with Lemony
Sour Cream, 90–91
Shrimp
Caesar Salad with Lemongrass-Skewered
Shrimp and Scallops, 70, 72
Glazed Shrimp with Bourbon Barbecue
Dunk, 39

Skewers
soaking, 11
threading, 11
types of, 13, 15
Smoked Duck with Spiced Apricots and
Watercress, 58
Smoked Salmon, Cream Cheese, and Martini
Onion Roulades, 66
Smoked Turkey, Avocado, and Bacon with
Blue Cheese Vinaigrette, 43
Smoky Black Bean Dip, 47
Snow peas
Lacquered Pork with Water Chestnuts and
Snow Peas, 51
Snow Pea Diamonds and Red Bell Pepper
Squares, 54
Spanish Olive and Cream Cheese Spheres on
Red Pepper Squares, 62
Spiced Pork with Plums, Roasted Garlic, and
Bay Leaves, 81
Spicy Tofu with Cilantro and Smoky Black
Bean Dip, 47
Spinach and Curried Pimiento Cheese
Pinwheels, 63
Spinach Tortellini with Roasted Red Pepper
Pesto, 49
Squash
Mushroom, Red Pepper, and Squash
Yakitori, 82, 84
Roasted Yellow Squash and Zucchini with
Green Onion and Basil Dip, 53
Strawberries
Frozen Strawberry Daiquiris, 108
Glazed Strawberry Shortcakes with
Lemony Sour Cream, 90–91
Sugarcane
Coconut Tapioca Custard with Tropical
Fruits and Apricot Syrup, 92
as skewers, 13
Sun-Dried Tomato Aioli, 69
Sweet Potato and Marshmallow Stix, 102
Swordfish, Moroccan-Spiced, with Red
Peppers and Lemon Drizzle, 27

T

Tapioca Custard, Coconut, with Tropical
Fruits and Apricot Syrup, 92
Techniques, 11–12
Tofu, Spicy, with Cilantro and Smoky Black
Bean Dip, 47

Tomatoes
Balsamic Sun-Dried Tomatoes, Broccoli,
and Smoked Gouda, 33
Broccoli Florets and Cherry Tomatoes, 54
Cherry Tomatoes, Marinated Artichoke
Hearts, and Mozzarella, 64
Sun-Dried Tomato Aioli, 69
Tortellini, Spinach, with Roasted Red Pepper
Pesto, 49
Tortillas
Curried Pimiento Cheese and Spinach
Pinwheels, 63
Peanut Butter, Rice Krispie, and Chocolate
Chip Roll-ups, 105
Smoked Salmon, Cream Cheese, and
Martini Onion Roulades, 66
Tuna with Black Olives and Marinated
Artichoke Crowns, 48
Turkey (Smoked), Avocado, and Bacon with
Blue Cheese Vinaigrette, 43

V

Vegetables, 54. *See also individual vegetables*
Vinaigrettes
Blue Cheese Vinaigrette, 43
Lime–Poppy Seed Vinaigrette, 61

W

Water Chestnuts, Lacquered Pork with Snow
Peas and, 51
Watermelon
Peppery Bacon-Wrapped Watermelon
Rind Pickles, 44
Watermelon and Blueberry Popsicles, 104
White Toblerone Fondue with Kiwi and
Pineapple Picks, 98

Y

Yakitori, Mushroom, Red Pepper, and
Squash, 82, 84
Yellow Curry Sauce, 69

Z

Zucchini and Yellow Squash, Roasted, with
Green Onion and Basil Dip, 53

The exact equivalents in the following tables have been rounded for convenience.

LIQUID/DRY MEASURES

U.S.	METRIC
¼ teaspoon	1.25 milliliters
½ teaspoon	2.5 milliliters
1 teaspoon	5 milliliters
1 tablespoon (3 teaspoons)	15 milliliters
1 fluid ounce (2 tablespoons)	30 milliliters
¼ cup	60 milliliters
⅓ cup	80 milliliters
½ cup	120 milliliters
1 cup	240 milliliters
1 pint (2 cups)	480 milliliters
1 quart (4 cups, 32 ounces)	960 milliliters
1 gallon (4 quarts)	3.84 liters
1 ounce (by weight)	28 grams
1 pound	454 grams
2.2 pounds	1 kilogram

LENGTH

U.S.	METRIC
⅛ inch	3 millimeters
¼ inch	6 millimeters
½ inch	12 millimeters
1 inch	2.5 centimeters

OVEN TEMPERATURE

FAHRENHEIT	CELSIUS	GAS
250	120	½
275	140	1
300	150	2
325	160	3
350	180	4
375	190	5
400	200	6
425	220	7
450	230	8
475	240	9
500	260	10